Famous Rifles and Machine Guns

General Editor

A. J. R. CORMACK

Published by
PROFILE PUBLICATIONS LTD.
Windsor, Berkshire, England.

© *Profile Publications Ltd.* 1977
ISBN 0 214 20325 5

First published in 1977 by
PROFILE PUBLICATIONS LIMITED
Dial House, Park St, Windsor, Berkshire, England

Printed in England by
GPS (Print) Limited

Contents

Acknowledgements

The editor would like to thank the following for their help without which this volume would not have been possible. Herb Woodend of the Pattern Room at Enfield, the manufacturer's Armalite, H&K, Erma SIG, Winchester and Auto Ordnance, the authors John Weeks and the late Frank Hobart.

Foreword

Many of the weapons in this volume have made their names on the battlefields of the world, others are famous from another era and the rest are current equipment of the armies of today.

The Winchester rifle needs little introduction as one of the weapons that helped to tame the West. It was said that you could load it on Sunday and shoot for the rest of the week! The impact of a reliable repeating rifle on the soldier and the cowboy who up till that time had had only a single shot to count must have been only a little less than the shock of the receiving renegades and bandits. The famous '66 and '73 as well as all the later models including the little known Winchester revolvers are described by John Weeks.

Still in use and preferred to its successor, the Bren gun has done sterling service with the soldiers of the British army. Based on a Czeckoslovakian design modified at Enfield, the Bren became the best light machine gun of its time, indeed, some say ever. The late Major Hobart describes the development of this weapon. The combination of accurate fire, interchangeable barrels and quick to change magazines made it the soldier's friend. This is surely the ultimate compliment for a military weapon.

The submachine gun, although developed earlier came into its own in the Second WW. The Erma company although they have had little success with the range of submachine guns that they developed during the 1950's and 1960's did produce the weapon that was as popular with those that used it as it was unpopular with those that did not. The MP40, or as it was erroneously known the Smeisser, was a milestone in the development of the submachine gun.

The roaring twenties brought many things which are well remembered, not the least of those is the Thompson submachine gun. While never achieving the vast production of many similar weapons, the Thompson with its large calibre .45ACP cartridge was still in use in Vietnam and is still offered for sale commercially. Details of all the development from the over complex original to the simplified WWII production along with the rare BSA guns are detailed.

The Soviet Union has produced in excess of ten million submachine guns, more than any other Nation. The loss of production facilities started the trend during WWII and even led to the formation of special squads who rode to battle on tanks armed only with submachine guns. The late Frank Hobart has covered in detail the development of these cheap, reliable and unsophisticated weapons which although they are no longer front line weapons with the Soviet forces still equip many irregular forces.

The firm of Heckler and Koch rose from the ruins of the old Mauser factories destroyed at the insistence of the Russians at the end of WWII. Starting by manufacturing sewing machine parts, then parts and gauges for the machine tool industry, the firm then progressed onto the manufacture under contract of parts of the G3 rifle. A contract from the German government for production of the complete G3 followed and with the future secure the firm branched out into a number of developments of the basic roller delayed blowback system. A range of weapons which have been supplied all over the world is currently in production.

When the name of SIG is mentioned amongst the experts in the field of small arms, the inevitable reaction is "If only we could all afford that quality". The best always costs more and SIG have the reputation of only producing the best. All their present production of weapons even those for military use have that extra finish and a look of rugged dependability that inspires one with the upmost confidence.

With a production now of over four million the M16 rifle has become a battle proven success. The M16 is however only one of the Armalite designed weapons that have achieved success. The Costa Mesa firm have produced design after design and the development of the M16, the AR18 is now in production in the UK by the firm of Sterling Armament. Armalite have been true pioneers in the development of the modern light weight small calibre rifle.

A. J. R. CORMACK

Index

LMG . . . Light Machinegun

MG . . . Machinegun

SMG . . . Submachine Gun

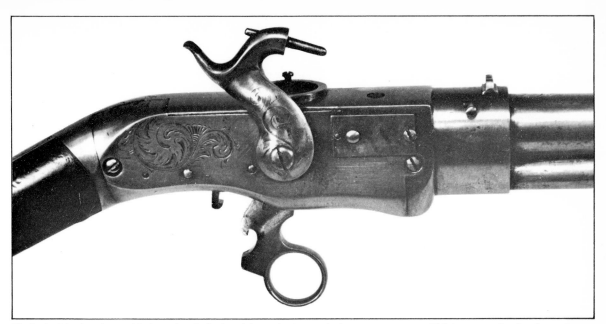

The lock of the Jennings, with the action cocked, and the under-lever at its foremost movement. This lever was also the trigger, there being a definite last pressure which fired the round. Note that in this specimen the pill magazine on top of the body is incomplete (*JSW*)

The Winchester Arms Company
by John Weeks

'Thet dam' Yankee rifle you can load on Sunday and shoot all week.'
Anon.

The story of the Wild West of the United States is a story compounded of a few simple items. Men, horses, cattle, sheep and guns. Guns that come in two forms, pistols or rifles. And these shoulder weapons are always Winchesters. For the Winchester Arms Company grew up with the great expansion of the Union, and in the romantic exploits of the cowboy, the Texas Ranger and the stage coach, the Winchester forms a permanent feature of the background, and often enough of the foreground too. But while today's portrayal of the Winchester usually concentrates on romance and highly-coloured battles, in fact it was actually the product of a careful, deliberate and highly skilful business operation directed by longsighted and imaginative financiers employing expert engineers . . . a story no less fascinating than the more popular one.
Oliver Fisher Winchester was born in Boston, Massachusetts on November 10th 1810. In July 1855 he was a successful shirt maker in New Haven, Connecticut, and he bought some stock in the Volcanic Arms Company. This company purchased the assets and patent rights of the former Smith and Wesson Company which manufactured the Volcanic guns, and production of that company's weapons continued under the new name. The Volcanic principle was the forerunner of the present cartridge in that the propellant and bullet were in one piece for loading. The bullet had a cavity in the base in which was the propellant and a percussion compound. Thus, the propellant would go off when struck by a firing pin, but it was naturally a weak charge and needed a light bullet. Sales fell despite continuous advertising and the company went bankrupt in 1857 to be purchased entirely by Oliver Winchester. The name was changed to The New Haven Arms Company and in 1858 a young shop superintendent named B. Tyler Henry was set the task of making a satisfactory metal cartridge. In short order he produced the ·44 rim fire, and altered the mechanism of the Volcanic to take it. In this he continued the one outstanding feature common to the Smith and Wesson, Volcanic and New Haven weapons, which was a tubular magazine running under the barrel, a

1

The 1849 Jennings Rifle. The first rifle ever to use the under-lever action to operate a repeater mechanism. It was the forerunner of the Volcanic, and used the same sort of ammunition (*JSW*)

lever action and a self cocking action combined with a small bolt. Henry left most of this as it was, and added an extractor. The rifle handled the ·44 cartridge very easily, and the magazine carried fifteen rounds. A rapid rate of fire could be maintained, firing a bullet of reasonable energy and striking power, and the system remained pre-eminent in American repeating rifles until the coming of the bolt action magazine loader. Unfortunately, it was hardly used in the Civil War, but enjoyed wide popularity among hunters.

The fortunes of the Company were built on Henry's patent, and the rifles were marketed under that name. Another change of location, and of Company title finally established the Winchester Repeating Arms Company on March 30th 1867.

Model 1866

A weak point of the Henry weapons was the slotted tubular magazine which was prone to damage and vulnerable to mud and dirt. A patent by Nelson King in 1866 incorporated a spring-closed loading port in the right side of the frame, and a closed magazine tube. Loading was faster than with the Henry Model, and there was little chance of jamming from dirt. Rounds could be inserted one by one with ease, with the rifle held at the point of balance in the other hand while so doing. The firm's catalogue claimed a continuous rate of fire of thirty shots a minute without great effort, whereas the best that was apparently achieved with the Henry system was 120 shots in nearly 6 minutes, or twenty a minute. Early models had iron receivers, but after a very few thousand the iron was replaced by brass and the name 'Winchester' appeared instead of Henry. This rifle had great success, being made until 1898, and sold in Europe as well as USA, but by 1872 it was apparent that a centre-fire rifle of greater power was needed.

Model 1873

This model was destined to become the most famous of all the Winchesters, and for years to talk of a 'Winchester' was to mean a model '73. It was the first centre-fire firearm from the Company for the reason that the rim fire ammunition was limited in its power by the fact that the cartridge case had to be of a sufficiently thin and soft metal to allow the rim to be crushed by the firing pin. Increasing the powder load led to ruptured cases, and this quickly spelt the end

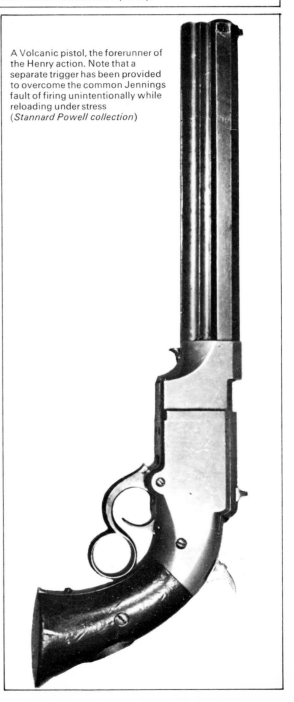

A Volcanic pistol, the forerunner of the Henry action. Note that a separate trigger has been provided to overcome the common Jennings fault of firing unintentionally while reloading under stress (*Stannard Powell collection*)

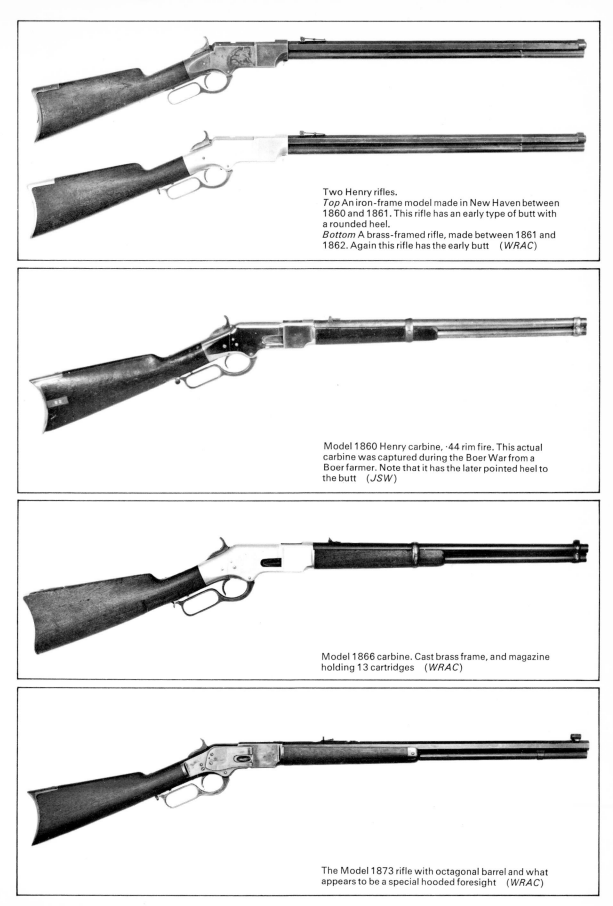

Two Henry rifles.
Top An iron-frame model made in New Haven between 1860 and 1861. This rifle has an early type of butt with a rounded heel.
Bottom A brass-framed rifle, made between 1861 and 1862. Again this rifle has the early butt   *(WRAC)*

Model 1860 Henry carbine, ·44 rim fire. This actual carbine was captured during the Boer War from a Boer farmer. Note that it has the later pointed heel to the butt   *(JSW)*

Model 1866 carbine. Cast brass frame, and magazine holding 13 cartridges   *(WRAC)*

The Model 1873 rifle with octagonal barrel and what appears to be a special hooded foresight   *(WRAC)*

A beautifully preserved specimen of the Model 1873
'One of One Thousand'. There is a non-standard
target backsight on the small of the butt   (*WRAC*)

A sectioned '73 Winchester rifle. The
magazine can be clearly seen with
rounds lying nose against tail and being
forced back towards the breech by the
magazine spring. Also visible is the
in-line toggle levers which lock the
breech, and the tray which will lift the
next round up into line with the chamber
(*Smithsonian Institution*)

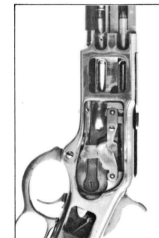

The '1 of 1000' marking
on the barrel of the rifle
in the above picture
(*WRAC*)

Model 1876 musket, a rare weapon. This type of musket was used by the Turkish Army in their victorious battle with the Russians at Plevna in 1877 (*JSW*)

The Model 1876 carbine, the standard model with the 22in. barrel. Calibre 45-75   (*WRAC*)

The breech of the Model 1876, showing the ejection slide open and the hammer cocked. This particular gun has a saddle ring, and in the photograph there is a museum tag hanging from it (*JSW*)

of the rimfire era. It differed very little in outline from the 1866 model, but the greater power of the ammunition gave it more striking energy, and by a happy chance Colt introduced in 1878 their single action army revolvers chambered for the same round (44-40 Winchester). The two weapons were a perfect complementary pair, each rugged and reliable, each doing a different job, and each using the same ammunition. Carried in a saddle bucket holster, the Winchester accompanied the horseman of the West throughout the troublesome final decades of the nineteenth century and earned its place in history and legend. The model was a success from the start of its introduction, and it did much to establish the high reputation of the Company. Over 720,000 had been made when the model was discontinued in 1919. Later versions of the '73 were made in ·38 WCF and ·32 WCF, the latter presumably as light sporting rifles. The '73 model also introduced a novel idea of selecting specially accurate barrels and setting them up into guns with set triggers and a special finish to be sold at a higher price. These were the legendary 'One of One Thousand' for which $100·00 was asked. The second grade of barrel was marked 'One of One Hundred' and fetched $20 above its normal price. The advertisement and fame of this selection system did wonders for the sales of all types of Winchesters.

Model 1876

Despite the success of the '73 model it was soon apparent that yet another redesign was going to be necessary if Winchester was to keep ahead of its competitors. They were offering single-shot weapons of considerable power, firing large cartridges, and were beginning to look at their own ideas for repeaters also. The continual demand for greater striking power led the firm to produce a 45-75 centre fire round. The bullet weighed 350 grains and was propelled by 75 grains of black powder, giving it more than double the energy of the model '73. In effect it was a stronger and slightly larger '73. It was a popular gun with those who needed a powerful repeater, and large numbers were sold in its short life, many of them overseas, as either sporting or police weapons. Manufacture was stopped in 1897 when the market for black powder guns had practically ceased. During its life it was produced in 50-95 express, 45-60 WCF, and 40-60 WCF calibres. As with the model '73, selected accurate barrels were sold at an extra price. President Teddy Roosevelt was a great fan of Winchester '76 and was perfectly willing to say so in public. In his full and adventurous life as a hunter he used several of the firm's models and was always delighted with them. Another useful piece of publicity came from the Royal Canadian Mounted Police who were equipped with the model '76 as their official shoulder arm.

With such success from their three models the Winchester Company could well have been forgiven if they had concentrated their energies on keeping the '66, '73 and '76 in full production, but the firm was headed by an astute and shrewd man, and Oliver Winchester was quick to sense any trends in the market. He could gauge better than most what

his next product should be, and when it should appear. It was perhaps as well that his early life should have been in a tough commercial atmosphere rather than on a machine shop floor.

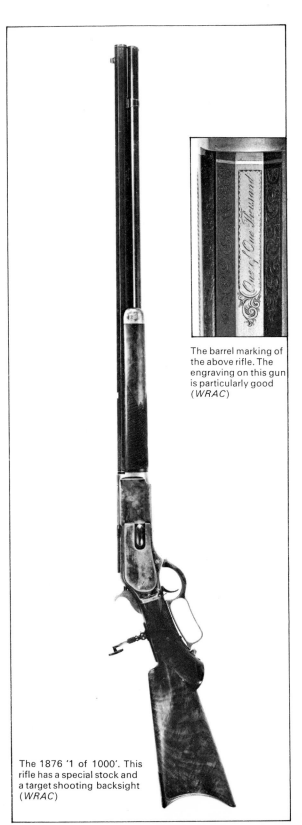

The barrel marking of the above rifle. The engraving on this gun is particularly good (*WRAC*)

The 1876 '1 of 1000'. This rifle has a special stock and a target shooting backsight (*WRAC*)

The Winchester pistols

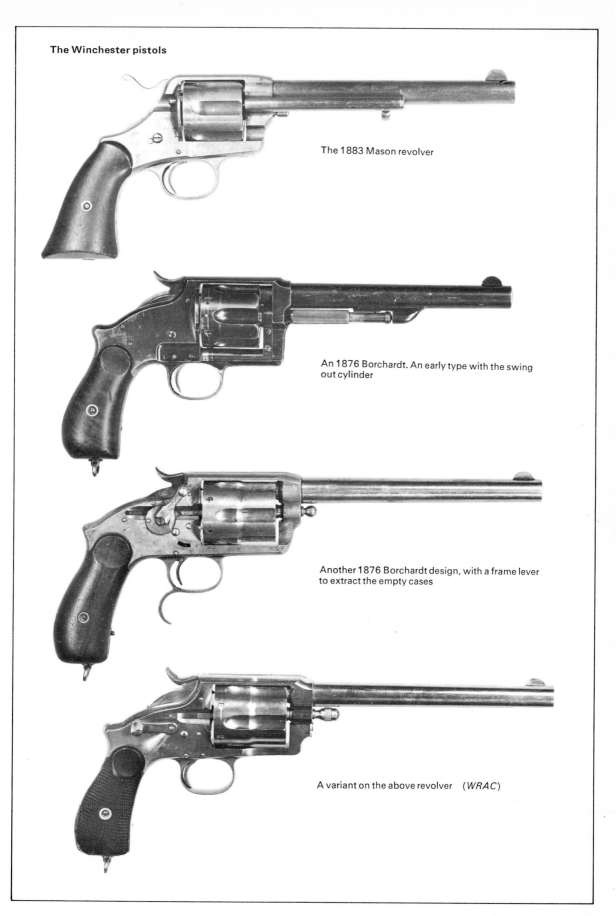

The 1883 Mason revolver

An 1876 Borchardt. An early type with the swing out cylinder

Another 1876 Borchardt design, with a frame lever to extract the empty cases

A variant on the above revolver   (*WRAC*)

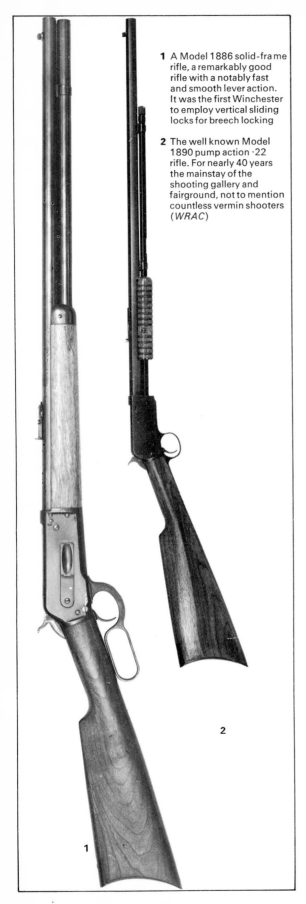

1 A Model 1886 solid-frame rifle, a remarkably good rifle with a notably fast and smooth lever action. It was the first Winchester to employ vertical sliding locks for breech locking

2 The well known Model 1890 pump action ·22 rifle. For nearly 40 years the mainstay of the shooting gallery and fairground, not to mention countless vermin shooters (*WRAC*)

Gun design moved fast in the 1870's, and by 1880 the pressure from competitors such as Remington was increasing. Their single shot guns were selling well, and there was talk of several firms trying their hands at making repeaters. Winchester replied by designing a wider range of weapons, and by looking at their own repeaters to see how they could be improved.

The Winchester Pistols

The first Winchester pistols were made in 1876, designed by Hugo Borchardt, who came to Winchester from the Colt Patent Arms Company. He remained with Winchester until about 1880, when he left for the Sharps Company, and later for Germany where he brought out his famous automatic pistols. His Winchester design was a single action model with a modern looking swing out cylinder holding six of the then new 44-40 rounds and a neat extractor. Another model was slightly shorter and stockier, with a side lever extractor. Whatever the reason, the revolvers were not continued and no more appeared until 1883 when another ex-employee of Colt's, one William Mason, produced an improved Borchardt type, but with side rod ejector. The cylinder and barrel remained the same. Again the calibre was 44-40, but this time the design looked very like the then current Colt Single Action Army Revolver, also known as the Frontier Model. Whether it was a nervousness of marketing almost a copy of the Colt, or simply a reluctance to enter the pistol field with no former experience to guide the firm is not now known, but Winchester made no more, and none were offered for sale. The excursion had been brief, and it was never revived. However legend has it that a 'deal' was made with Colt that Winchester would make no revolvers if Colt made no rifles.

Model 1886

The interest in pistols had not been allowed to affect research into better repeater shoulder arms, and in 1885 a new one was ready for the market. Although outwardly much the same as the previous ones, it was far stronger and fired the heavy ·45 military cartridge of that time. The design was by another well known name in gun making history, this time John Moses Browning, whom Winchester hired on contract. He went on to design many other Winchesters until he left for Belgium in 1902. The model 1886 had several changes in its locking mechanism to withstand the higher pressures, and was the first repeating rifle to successfully employ sliding vertical locks. The action was remarkably fast and smooth and it was generally considered the best of its kind ever made. The appearance of this excellent weapon had an immediate effect on the sales of the '73 and '76 models, and in its life it was offered with no less than ten alternative chamber sizes, ranging from ·50-110 to 33 WCF. It appeared in 1886 in the following forms : Sporting rifle with straight grip, Sporting rifle with pistol grip, Carbine, Musket with bayonet, and other varieties to special order. Actual manufacture was discontinued in 1935, by which date 159,994 had been made. An interesting point is that some of the early barrels of

1 The Model 1894 rifle, the so-called 'Klondike Model' from its popularity in the 1898 gold rush. This was Winchester's first repeater to be specifically designed for smokeless powders. It was also the first Winchester to pass the million mark, and No. 1,000,000 was presented to President Coolidge in 1927. It is still in production   (*WRAC*)

2 The Model 1892 44-40 rifle. A neat and handy weapon which was immensely popular in South America and Australia. This model was the second Winchester to pass the million mark, which occurred on 17 December 1932. Production ceased soon after, at a total of 1,004,067   (*JSW*)

3 A Model 1894 rifle fitted with a pistol grip stock   (*JSW*)

4 A Centennial Model 1894 30-30 calibre. This rifle is a presentation model, and the engraved plate on the butt is clearly visible   (*JSW*)

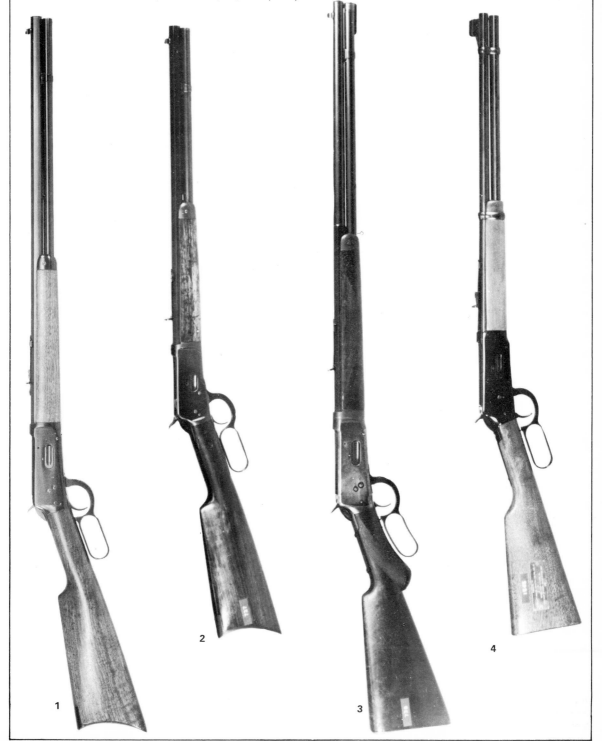

1

2

3

4

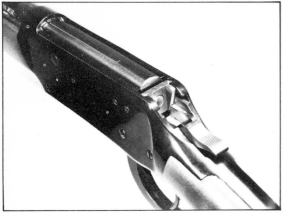

The breech of the Centennial Model 1894, with the action closed and the hammer cocked. The vertical locking slide can clearly be seen (*JSW*)

The breech of a Model 1894 44-40, action open and the feed tray in front of the chamber. If the magazine had been loaded a round would be placed precisely in position so that the bolt would ram it into the chamber on closing (*JSW*)

the Model 86 are marked 'Browning Bros. Ogden Utah'. This came about by Winchester agreeing to pay Browning part payment for the manufacturing rights in complete rifles.

Ammunition
Winchester realised very early on in his arms manufacturing career that any weapon was only as good as its ammunition, and with the introduction of the Henry rifle he laid down an ammunition plant. This plant produced various calibres of ammunition for the Union Army during the Civil War, and it continued to grow as the Winchester rifles sold. In 1871 a chemical ballistics laboratory and special plant was installed, and the design and production of ammunition continued hand in hand with guns, so that it soon became almost as important an income earner, and has remained so to this day.
By 1888 the department was experimenting with smokeless powders, and it soon became evident that the new propellant was going to mean that a whole new range of weapons would have to be produced to fire them. The old black powder guns would be obsolete on the day that the first of the new guns appeared, and Winchester undertook a huge research programme to investigate every aspect of ammunition and gun design and manufacture. It took time and others beat them to the post, but none

had the resources and expertise of Winchester : it was not until 1895 that the first smokeless powder cartridge came out of the factory, but the sales effort behind it was enormous, and by 1900 Winchester could, and did, supply a sporting gun for literally every requirement from target shooting to big game hunting. The range covered 15 different guns, 2 single-shot rifles, 10 repeating rifles, and 3 shot guns. The smallest rifle was a single-shot bolt action ·22 RF, which was not a great success and was soon dropped. The repeaters were mostly under-lever actions with tubular magazines, but not all were that type.

Model 1890
This rifle was the first Winchester repeater of the slide or trombone action, and was the most popular ·22 RF repeater ever produced by the firm. It was another of John Browning's contract designs, and it continued to be made until 1932, when it was replaced by the very similar Model 62. Model 62 lasted until 1958 when Model 63 succeeded it and remained in production until 1963 when the last trombone ·22 RF repeater was made. 73 years is a good run for any type of firearm, and the last model was not strikingly dissimilar from the first, a wonderful testimony to Browning's design acumen. The old trombone rifles were for years the standard equipment of shooting galleries the world over. The 1890 slide action was the first of many variations which were to appear in the following years in a wide variety of calibres.

Model 1894
The cream of the crop of the guns of 1900 was undoubtedly the Model 1894, by far the best-selling rifle yet made in the Winchester factory. This again was a Browning design, and it was announced in November 1894 with these words in the catalogue : 'We believe that no repeating rifle system ever made will appeal to the eye and understanding of the rifleman as this will and that use will continue to warrant first impressions.'
The prophecy has come true indeed. This lever action model soon became famous all over the world, and is still being manufactured today, more than three million guns and seventy-seven years later. The Model 94 was the first of the factory's repeaters to be especially designed for the smokeless powders which by 1900 were being made in large quantities by the WRAC but when the Model 94 first appeared there was some delay in the cartridge production, and the early models were chambered for the 32-40 and 38-55 black-powder rounds. However, the 1895 catalogue lists 25-35 and 30-30 barrels, these in nickel steel, for the smokeless propellant.

The Company forged ahead in the early years of the century, and in 1903 the first Winchester semi-automatic rifle was added to the range. This was claimed as the first ever semi-automatic rifle to be made and marketed in the United States, and it was offered in ·22 RF only. It worked by blow back action, the bolt being sufficiently heavy to keep the breech closed until the bullet had left the barrel, when it started to move back and carry out the

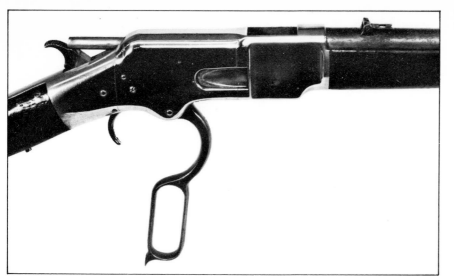

The action of the Model 1866, open   (*JSW*)

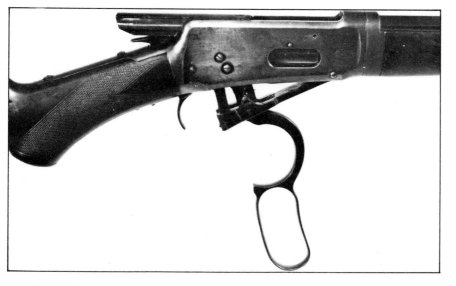

The action of the Model 1892, open   (*JSW*)

The action of the Model 1894, open   (*JSW*)

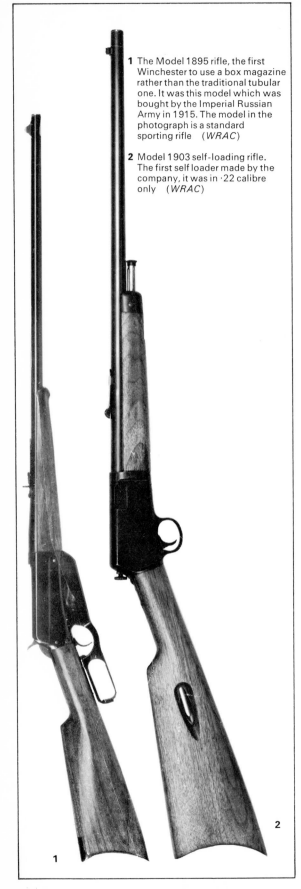

1 The Model 1895 rifle, the first Winchester to use a box magazine rather than the traditional tubular one. It was this model which was bought by the Imperial Russian Army in 1915. The model in the photograph is a standard sporting rifle (*WRAC*)

2 Model 1903 self-loading rifle. The first self loader made by the company, it was in ·22 calibre only (*WRAC*)

3 Model 1910 self-loading rifle. Calibre 401 Winchester self loading cartridge (*WRAC*)

4 Model 52 ·22 rifle. The one illustrated is a Jaeger, made after 1937 when the safety catch was moved from the left to the right side. First offered to the public in 1919, the model 52 is still made (*WRAC*)

1 Model 54 Supergrade bolt-action rifle. This model first appeared in 1925, and has been made in at least ten different calibres from 30-06 Springfield to 22 Hornet. In 1936 the '54 was succeeded by the Model 70, which was an up-dated version of the '54; it is still made (*WRAC*)

2 The Model 61 slide-action repeating rifle, ·22 calibre. Introduced in 1932 to up date the Model 1890, the 61 was hammerless and smoother to operate than the '90. The last ones were made in 1963 (*WRAC*)

3 Model 88 lever action sporting rifle. Box magazine holding four rounds, hammerless action. A very strong, light rifle utilising the traditional under lever, and apart from commemorative models the last Winchester to feature the action (*WRAC*)

re-loading cycle. It stayed in production until 1932 when it was redesigned and reissued as the Model 63, chambered for the long rifle ·22 cartridge. Model 63 remained in production until 1958, by which time about 300,000 of the two models had been made. Sales were not brisk with the Model 03 since sportsmen were hardly ready for such an innovation, but they were sufficiently encouraging to try a larger version in 1905, the Model 05 in ·32 and ·35 WCF sizes. Due to the cost of this weapon and the comparatively low velocity cartridges used in it, it was never a successful model, and only about 30,000 were sold.

By 1912 the Company was really flourishing, and in the ammunition plant every part of the product was made in the factory even to the lead shot for the shotgun ammunition, and for this a 170-foot tower had had to be built. The Company employed 6,000 men and sold 30,000 sporting arms every year. Modern transport was taking hunters to wider and wider regions, and the general rising of standards of living led to increasing leisure activities such as skeet and target shooting.

It all changed in 1914. The War trebled the work force in the plant, and increased the floor space. Instead of sporting guns Winchester made Enfields, Brownings and other military models, as well as their ammunition. 250,000 Pattern 14 and 550,000 Pattern 17 Enfields were made, as well as 300,000 Model 95 Winchester muskets for Imperial Russia, surely the last time any Regular army

bought a lever action repeater in quantity.

Despite the boost of the war, the 1920's were a hard time. Money was scarce and Winchester made over 750 different hardware products even turning to refrigerators for one unprofitable spell. The Wall Street crash almost finished the Company, it being saved by John Olin, of the Western Cartridge Company. The two merged, and the combination was able to expand and continue production.

So Winchester guns carried on, and three new shotguns appeared in 1920. Other arms were produced at later intervals, notably the Model 52 rifle, the Model 54 bolt action rifle and the Model 21 double barrel shotgun. By 1940 twenty-three new guns had been introduced, five of them shotguns, and eighteen rifles. One of them was the Model 70 bolt action sporting rifle, still in production today, in seven styles and eleven calibres; but once again military weapons took over the plant, and until 1945 the firm made both the M1 rifle and the M1 ·30 carbine. The latter weapon was developed by Winchester engineers, and over 800,000 were made in the factory. All told Winchester made 1·3 million military weapons and 15 billion rounds of ammunition during the war, and, as before, the plant had to be expanded to cope with the demands. Since 1945 the firm has returned to making sporting models with a much happier financial background than the one which dogged after World War 1. Today it continues to be a leader in its field, just as it has always been.

The Model 70 bolt-action rifle, a beautifully finished and balanced game hunting and long range accuracy rifle   (*WRAC*)

Winchester Shotguns

The sale of shotguns started early in the history of the Winchester. In 1878 the firm imported a quantity of English shotguns and sold them under the Winchester name. The business was so profitable and brisk that it was decided to manufacture them in New Haven. After considerable thought a patent of John Browning's was bought and marketed in 1887 as the first lever action repeating shotgun to be made in USA. It was produced in 10 and 12 bore, with little or no decoration, and a capacity of four cartridges in the magazine and one on the carrier. It was of generous build, which led to a weight of 9lb

in the 10 bore model, but it was robust and reliable.

By 1890 competition from other manufacturers forced Winchester to bring out another model, and again a patent of Browning's was used for the pilot design. This time the repeating action was by a sliding forearm, or 'trombone' action, and the gun came out in 1893. It was withdrawn in 1897 as it could not withstand the new smokeless powders, and its successor, the Model 1897, was continued until 1957. It is still encountered in large numbers today, over 1 million having been made.

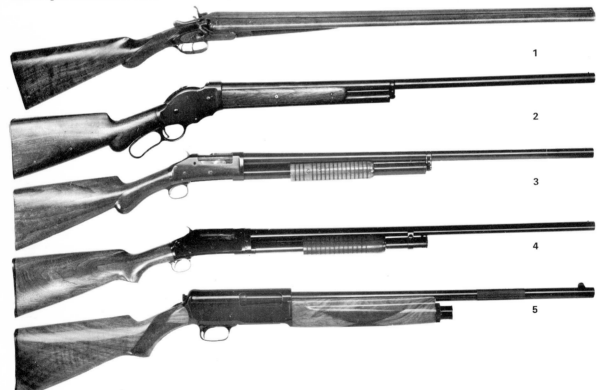

1

2

3

4

5

1 English made double barrel shotgun, sold through the New York store of the company from 1879 to 1884   (*WRAC*)

2 The Model 1887 lever action shotgun, the first lever action shotgun to be made in the USA. Magazine capacity, four shells   (*WRAC*)

3 Model 1893 slide action shotgun, based on a design of John Browning. Made only in 12 gauge, it was for black powder propellants   (*WRAC*)

4 The Model 1897 shotgun was an improved model 1893, and was more than strong enough for smokeless powders. It continued to be made until 1957, by when 10,247,000 had been sold   (*WRAC*)

5 The Model 1911 self-loading shotgun. The action was operated by recoil, and several changes had to be made to the first models before the system was satisfactory. World War 1 then upset sales, and the Model 1911 was discontinued in 1925   (*WRAC*)

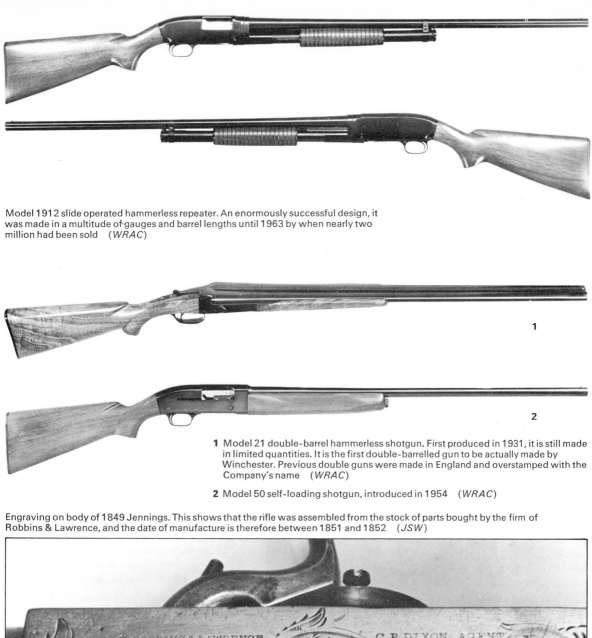

Model 1912 slide operated hammerless repeater. An enormously successful design, it was made in a multitude of gauges and barrel lengths until 1963 by when nearly two million had been sold (*WRAC*)

1

2

1 Model 21 double-barrel hammerless shotgun. First produced in 1931, it is still made in limited quantities. It is the first double-barrelled gun to be actually made by Winchester. Previous double guns were made in England and overstamped with the Company's name (*WRAC*)

2 Model 50 self-loading shotgun, introduced in 1954 (*WRAC*)

Engraving on body of 1849 Jennings. This shows that the rifle was assembled from the stock of parts bought by the firm of Robbins & Lawrence, and the date of manufacture is therefore between 1851 and 1852 (*JSW*)

Close up of the engraving on the butt tang of the Model 1894   (*JSW*)

Magazine opening of the Jennings rifle   (*JSW*)

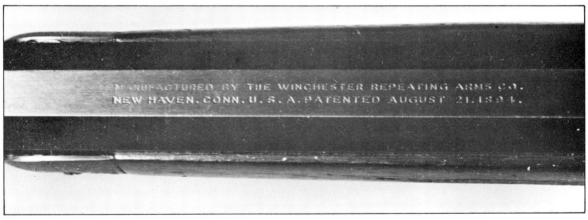

Close up of engraving on barrel of Model 1894   (*JSW*)

Self-Loading Shotgun Model 1911

After much trouble in the design, a self-loading shotgun was brought out in 1911, but it was never a commercial success, despite its novel recoil operation and five round magazine. In 1912 Winchester went back to the slide action for their **Model 1912** with a hammerless action. It was enormously successful, almost 2 million having been made by the time production ceased in 1963. It was offered in a huge variety of types, gauges, chambers, chokes and weights to suit all tastes ; for years it was known as the Perfect Repeater and used for small game shooting everywhere.

After World War 1 some cheap single-shot weapons were sold, but they never enjoyed a great popularity, and were perhaps a mistake for a firm which normally only made precision arms. The next step was the **Model 21** Double Barrel which appeared in 1931. As with the Model 12 a wide variety of options was offered from 28 bore to 12 bore, and with single or double triggers. It is a gun of the highest quality with remarkable shooting ability and great precision in its manufacture. It has gained an enviable name among shooters everywhere, and the proof of its excellence lies in the fact that it is still in production in three grades.

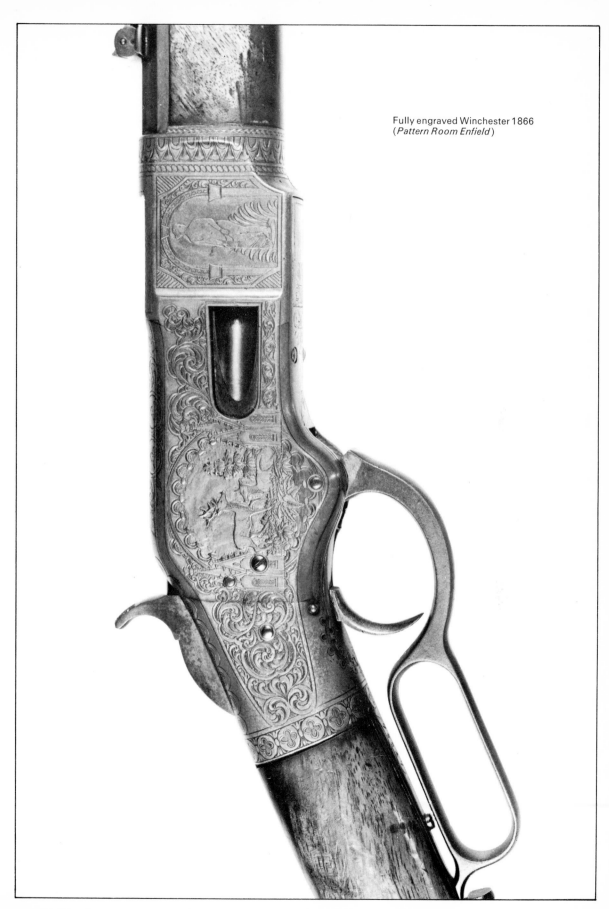

Fully engraved Winchester 1866
(*Pattern Room Enfield*)

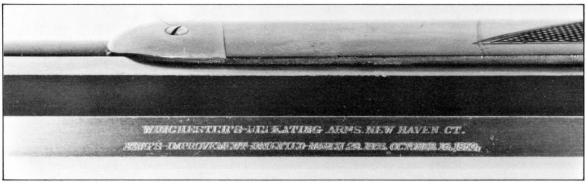

Barrel markings on the Winchester 1873   (*J. B. Hall*)

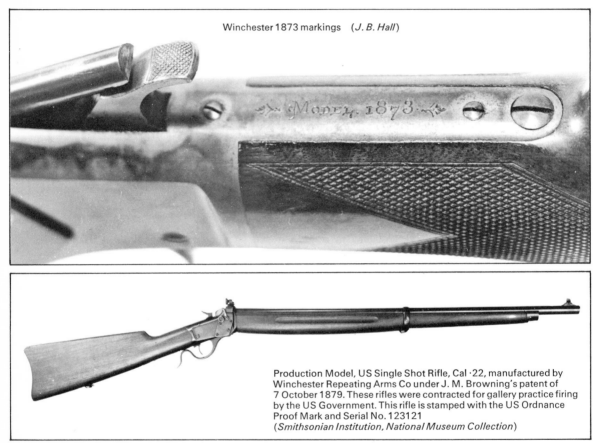

Winchester 1873 markings   (*J. B. Hall*)

Production Model, US Single Shot Rifle, Cal ·22, manufactured by Winchester Repeating Arms Co under J. M. Browning's patent of 7 October 1879. These rifles were contracted for gallery practice firing by the US Government. This rifle is stamped with the US Ordnance Proof Mark and Serial No. 123121 (*Smithsonian Institution, National Museum Collection*)

After World War 2 Winchester returned to the post war market with a slide-action repeater and another self loader. The latter was the **Model 50** which was introduced in 1954. It worked on the short recoil principle, in which the barrel remained fixed, and the floating chamber moved back a fraction of an inch to unlock the bolt and start it on its rearward move. It was an expensive gun, the receiver being milled from the solid, and the barrel bored from solid bar. Next came an over and under, the Model 101, and the Model 1200 slide action which locks its bolt by a rotating bolt head similar to a rifle. The latest is the Model 1400 automatic shotgun which works by gas operation in a very similar way to many semi-automatic rifles and machine guns. It is a very well finished, high quality gun in many different styles and sizes, and since 1966 a Recoil Reduction System

has been available which reduces the apparent recoil by 78%.

At all times the policy of the Company has been to design guns which the market needed, and to produce them in the highest possible quality at the price which the market could afford. It sounds like a classical formula for success, but it can only be achieved by continuous effort, rigorous control of the product, and a deep understanding of the needs of the shooter. For the last one hundred and five years gun users all over the world have had cause to be grateful that Winchester knew their business so well.

Small Arms Editor: A. J. R. Cormack

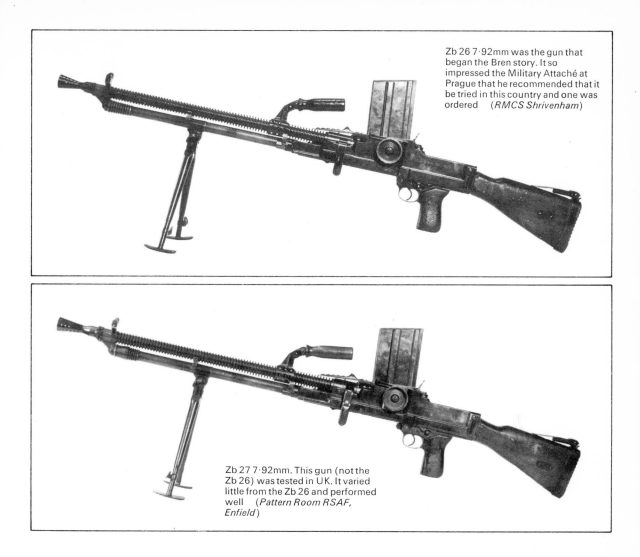

Zb 26 7·92mm was the gun that began the Bren story. It so impressed the Military Attaché at Prague that he recommended that it be tried in this country and one was ordered   (*RMCS Shrivenham*)

Zb 27 7·92mm. This gun (not the Zb 26) was tested in UK. It varied little from the Zb 26 and performed well   (*Pattern Room RSAF, Enfield*)

The Bren Gun

by Major F.W.A. Hobart (Retd)[1]

Introduction

When the 1914-1918 war ended the British Army possessed large quantities of the Vickers MMG Mk 1 and the Lewis gun. The Vickers gun was generally recognized as being the best gun of its kind in the world but the Lewis gun had several drawbacks. Its weight, its bulk, the nature of its feed system and its proneness to feed stoppages all made it unsatisfactory as the infantry section LMG and it was agreed that a replacement was required.

It was decided in 1922 that the Browning Automatic Rifle—somewhat modified—should be accepted into service as the Browning Light Machine Gun. This decision was never implemented in full and various sporadic trials of other LMGs were carried

out in a rather desultory way for some years. In December 1922 the Small Arms Committee arranged comparative trials of the Browning, Madsen, Beardmore-Farquhar, Hotchkiss and the Type 'D' Lewis Gun.[2] The trials of the Hotchkiss and Madsen, which were considered cavalry LMGs, were carried out by the 13th Hussars, the remainder by 1st Btn Dorset Regt. The Browning was considered to be the most suitable gun. In 1924 the Beardmore-Farquhar Mk II LMG was tried and rejected, and in 1925 the French Chatelleraut 7·5mm LMG was examined and in 1926 a Swiss Furrer LMG was purchased, tried, and 'no further trials recommended'. In 1927 the McCrudden LMG and Erikson LMG were examined

---

[2]SAC Minute No 555.

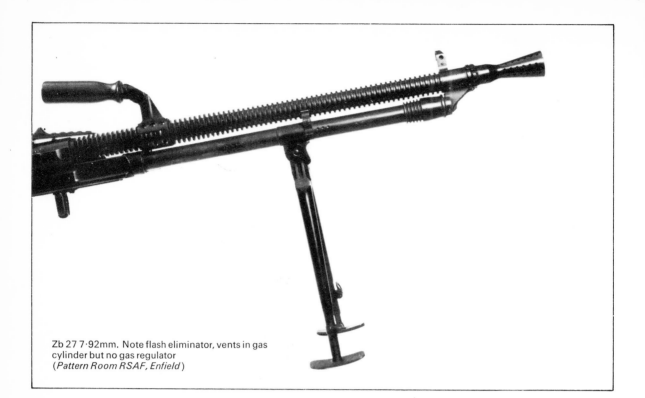
Zb 27 7·92mm. Note flash eliminator, vents in gas cylinder but no gas regulator
(*Pattern Room RSAF, Enfield*)

and in 1928 the new Madsen was tried. The McCrudden gun was resubmitted in 1929 but was not acceptable.

On 29 October 1930 comparative trials were arranged[1] for the Browning ·303 LMG, Darne ·303 LMG, Vickers-Berthier LMG, Kiralyi-Ende 7 LMG, the Madsen ·303 LMG and the Zb 26 LMG of 7·92mm calibre. Of these the Browning came from USA, Darne from France, Madsen from Denmark, the V-B was British made, the Kiralyi was made by SIG of Switzerland and the Zb came from Czechoslovakia. The Zb 26 came to the notice of the Small Arms Committee via a report from the MA at Prague. The cost of one Zb 26 for trial was £75 5s 0d and 10,000 rounds of 7·92mm ammunition cost £52 6s 8d. With a packing and delivery charge of £7 10s 4d the cost of equipment for the trial—which turned out to be of great importance—was £135 2s 0d. The MA at Prague also reported on the Kosar recoil reducer and stabilizer and a tripod fitted with this gear was ordered at a cost of £74.

In 1930 the decision was made to replace both the Vickers MMG Mk 1 and the Lewis Gun with one weapon capable of carrying out both roles.[2]

In view of this the date of the trials of the LMGs was brought forward and the weapons were fired as they became available. The Darne arrived too late for inclusion. The Czech firm of Ceskoslovenska Zbrojovka Akciova Spolecnost of Brno did *NOT* supply a Zb 26 as ordered but sent instead the Zb 27 which was an improved version. So the Zb 26 was never officially tried in this country. The complete record of the trial of the eight guns is in SAC Minute No 1108. In brief the tests were :

[1]SAC Minute No 1099.
[2]War Office Papers 20/Inf/2024.

Test
1 Examination, tests and functioning.
2 Accuracy trials.
3 Rate of fire trials.
4 Firing at elevation and depression.
5 Accuracy from hot barrels.
6 Accuracy trials (repeated).
7 Influence of fouling tests.
8 Functioning test of 1000 rounds combined with changing hot barrels.
9 Accuracy trials (repeated).
10 Accuracy from prone position. Firing from side, upside and down. Firing from hip on move.
11 Accuracy at full automatic fire.
12 Ease of handling when hot.
13 1000 rounds endurance—using 2 barrels.
14 Accuracy trials (repeated)
15 Visibility of flash.
16 Changing spare parts when the gun was hot.
17 Maximum and minimum speed of operation using regulator.
18 Grouping.
19 Tests for stoppages with damaged ammunition.
20 Endurance trial—2500 rounds.
21 Test of mounting and functioning.
22 Accuracy at 500 yards.
23 Grouping at 50 yards.
24 Stability of mounting.
25 Stability of mounting.
26 Accuracy at 500 yards.
27 MP1 from 4 different barrels.

After all this the comments were :

Vickers-Berthier
'A promising gun but requires further development and improvement in many details.'

Zb 27

'Functioning—excellent throughout. I doubt whether any other gun has ever passed through so many tests with us, giving so little trouble.'

The weapons were subsequently tested for functioning in mud and sand. The V-B and Zb 27 were satisfactory.

In a detailed summary of the mechanical features of the Zb 27 after firing 10986 rounds, the wear was described as 'negligible' and the barrel diameter had increased by 0·005in.

The V-B report was not so good but concluded 'These and other minor points are all remedial and properly developed it should be the equal of the Zb gun'.

The SAC recommended further trials.

In April 1931 the Zb 27 was ordered in ·303in calibre. The conversion was carried out on a Zb 30 and incorporated several small improvements over the Zb 27. In June 1931 the SAC recommended a programme of trials for the Zb 30, Vickers-Berthier and Darne. These consisted of

a Long range accuracy trials at Hythe consisting of three series of shoots at 500, 1000, 1500, 2000 to 2500 yards.

b Endurance trial at Enfield of 30,000 rounds.

c A special trial of a new heavy Vickers-Berthier Barrel.

Zb 27 7·92mm. Lettering on RHS of body
(*Pattern Room RSAF, Enfield*)

Zb 27 7·92mm. Lettering on LHS of body
(*Pattern Room RSAF, Enfield*)

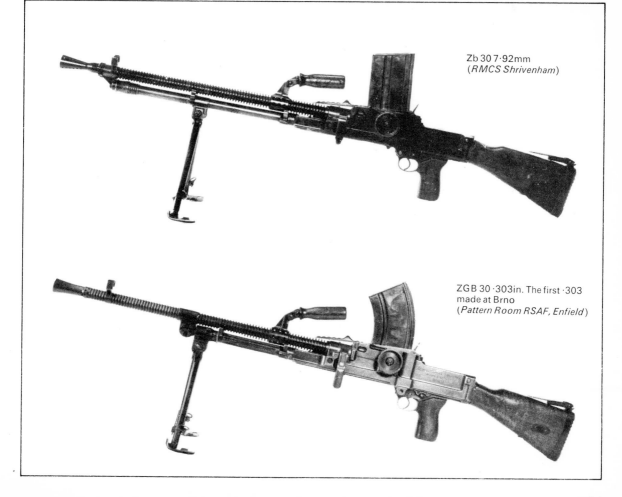

Zb 30 7·92mm
(*RMCS Shrivenham*)

ZGB 30 ·303in. The first ·303 made at Brno
(*Pattern Room RSAF, Enfield*)

The trial report (SAC Minute 1188) runs to 88 foolscap pages. It is one of the most interesting and comprehensive reports that one can imagine. The final conclusion on the Zb 30 was :

'That the Zb gun . . . is of such outstanding design, workmanship and material as to warrant further serious consideration.

Its performance during the trials has been remarkable having in view the fact that it was designed primarily for a rimless cartridge and a nitro-cellulose charge. The present defects of the weapon are :

a Excessive fouling due to the present position of the gas port which is not suitable for a cordite charge.

b Ejection is faulty due to the gun having been converted at short notice to fire the rimmed Mk VII ·303 cartridge.

In May 1932 Mr Staller of the Zb company took the gun back to Brno and it was modified by moving the gas block 9·65in towards the chamber, fitting a new gas block, cylinder and front half of the piston. The gun was brought to England by its designer Vaclav Holek. It was tested and 18,936 rounds were fired ; it functioned perfectly. During the 15,000 round endurance trial there were 90 stoppages ; 61 were caused by loose caps in the ammunition. The Committee asked for a 30 round magazine—instead of the 20 fitted and ordered 10 guns incorporating the improvements—and known as the ZGB—which with

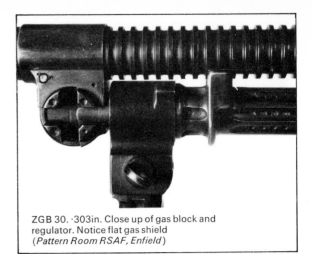

ZGB 30. ·303in. Close up of gas block and regulator. Notice flat gas shield
(*Pattern Room RSAF, Enfield*)

spare barrels, spare parts and accessories were to cost £175 per set. Whilst the ZGB guns were being made the Director of Munitions visited Brno between 14 January 1933 and 22 January 1933 and as a result of discussion with Mr Holek the designer and the Superintendent Royal Small Arms Factory, a Czech design change was incorporated to allow the piston buffer to take the recoil not only of the piston but of the barrel and body. This movement of about

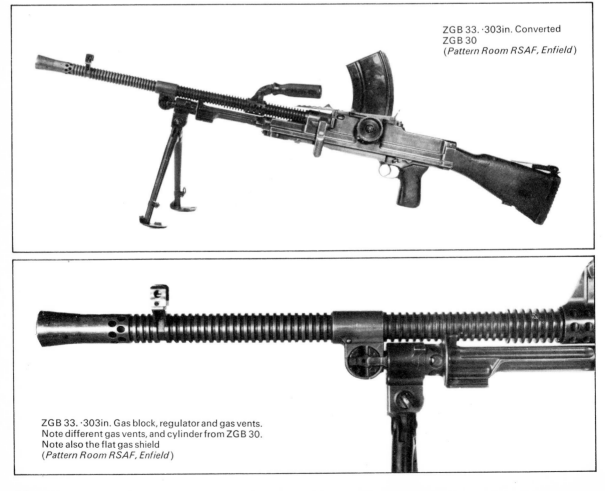

ZGB 33. ·303in. Converted ZGB 30
(*Pattern Room RSAF, Enfield*)

ZGB 33. ·303in. Gas block, regulator and gas vents. Note different gas vents, and cylinder from ZGB 30. Note also the flat gas shield
(*Pattern Room RSAF, Enfield*)

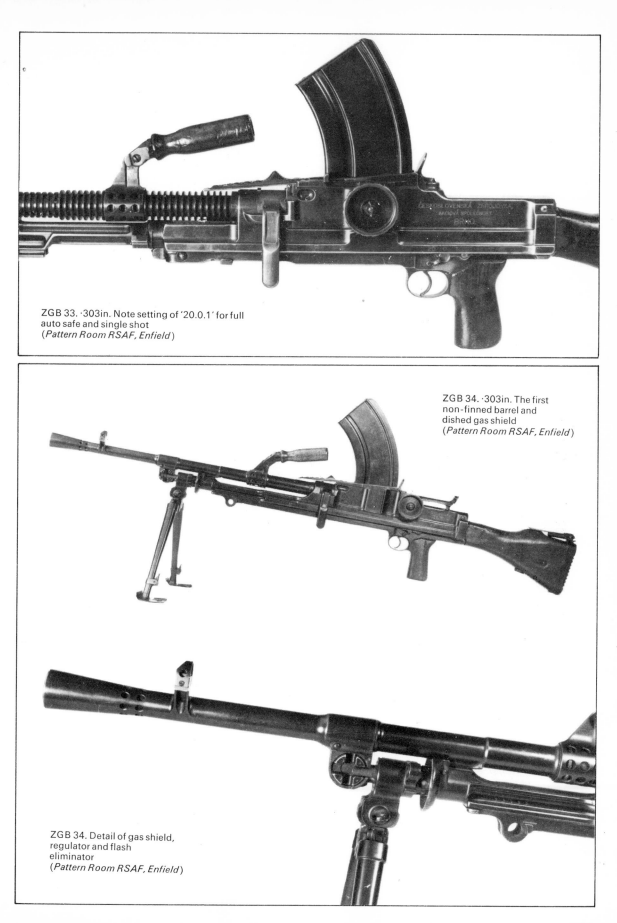

ZGB 33. ·303in. Note setting of '20.0.1' for full
auto safe and single shot
(*Pattern Room RSAF, Enfield*)

ZGB 34. ·303in. The first
non-finned barrel and
dished gas shield
(*Pattern Room RSAF, Enfield*)

ZGB 34. Detail of gas shield,
regulator and flash
eliminator
(*Pattern Room RSAF, Enfield*)

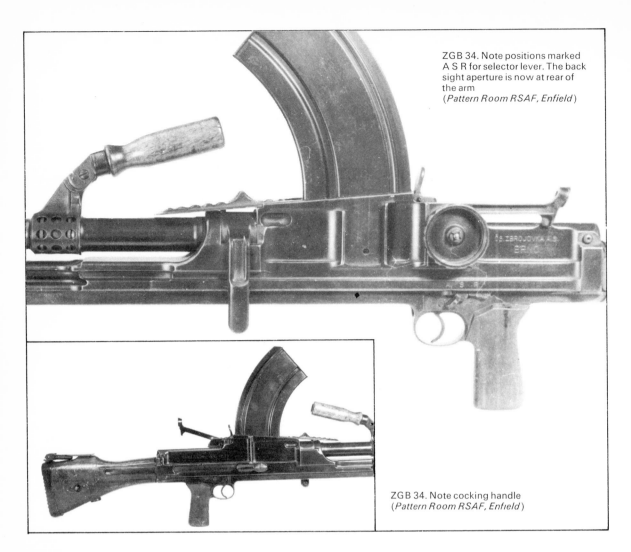

ZGB 34. Note positions marked A S R for selector lever. The back sight aperture is now at rear of the arm
(*Pattern Room RSAF, Enfield*)

ZGB 34. Note cocking handle
(*Pattern Room RSAF, Enfield*)

2mm reduced the recoil felt by the firer. The ZGB so modified was called the ZGB 32 and was given preliminary testing at Enfield by firing some 500 rounds and was then sent to Hythe for a 4000 round endurance test and finally fired a further 25,000 rounds at Enfield for functioning and wear. Whilst at Enfield a modified ejector designed as a chisel to burr brass over the cap and prevent 'caps out' was tried with complete success. The ZGB 32 was satisfactory but the committee decided further improvements were possible and should be incorporated in a modified version to be known as the ZGB 33. There were 25 modifications of which the most important were :

Speed of gun to be reduced from 600 rounds a minute to 480 rounds a minute.
Sights to read to 2000 yards by 50s.
No fins on barrel.
Length of barrel to be reduced by 1·9in.
Gas exhaust shield to be cupped.
Modified butt slide catch.
Modified cocking handle.
Modified comb to butt.
Lengthen idle movement of piston to delay breech opening.
New ejector.

Two of the ZGB 33s were ordered and an extra six spare barrels were also asked for so that the weapons could be tested :

Acceptance tests	1000 rounds
Endurance of mechanism	150,000 rounds
Accuracy and other tests	50,000 rounds

The trials were fired on 29 January 1934 with success. The speed of the gun was reduced, the locked period of the breech was increased, accuracy was improved and over 140,000 rounds were fired before any part failed.
Two models of the ZGB 33, known as the ZGB 34, were purchased on 14 April 1934. A 50,000 round endurance test was then fired in August 1934 to compare the ZGB 34 with the latest heavy barrelled Vickers-Berthier. This proved finally and conclusively that the Czech Zb was the better gun. This trial was reported at great length in SAC minute 1545. From this description it is clear that the Zb gun was extremely thoroughly tested and hundreds of thousands of rounds were fired before it was adopted.
The decision to use this gun to replace both the Vickers gun and the Lewis gun was rescinded in 1937 when it was expected that the Zb 53 air-cooled gun (later known as the BESA) of 7·92mm calibre

would replace the Vickers and the ZGB take over the light role.

When the acceptance committee expressed themselves as fully satisfied arrangements were made for the production of the gun at the Royal Small Arms Factory at Enfield. The gun was named the BREN from BRno and ENfield. The drawings had to be converted from metric measure to inches and this was completed in January 1935. During 1934 Mr Robinson the Factory Superintendent planned the production line, installed machine tools and the tool room started on the gauges. Some idea

First Bren Gun
Manufactured at
Royal Small Arms
Factory Enfield
And Fired Sept.3ᴿᴰ1937

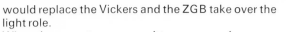

Mk 1 Bren. Close up of butt plate—Fig 16
(*Pattern Room RSAF, Enfield*)

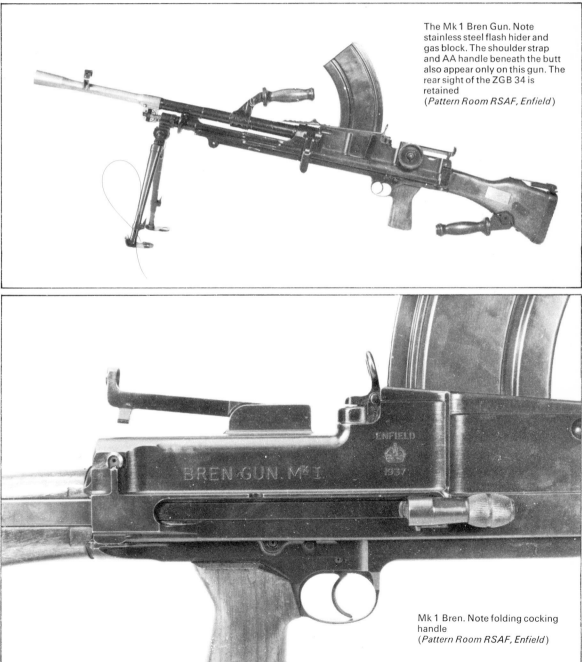

The Mk 1 Bren Gun. Note stainless steel flash hider and gas block. The shoulder strap and AA handle beneath the butt also appear only on this gun. The rear sight of the ZGB 34 is retained
(*Pattern Room RSAF, Enfield*)

Mk 1 Bren. Note folding cocking handle
(*Pattern Room RSAF, Enfield*)

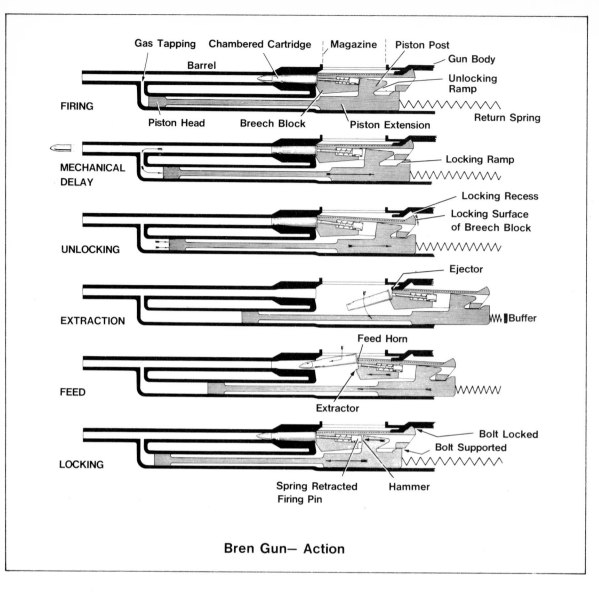

Bren Gun— Action

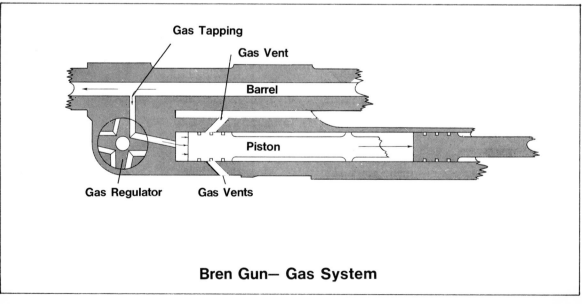

Bren Gun— Gas System

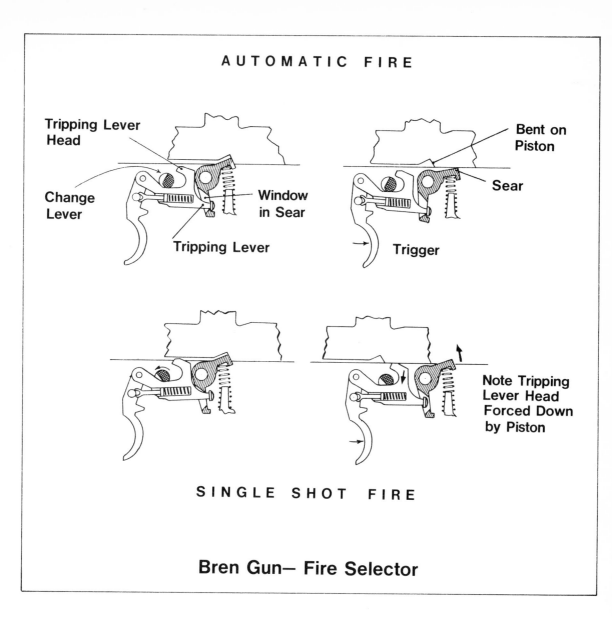

AUTOMATIC FIRE

Tripping Lever Head

Change Lever

Tripping Lever

Window in Sear

Bent on Piston

Sear

Trigger

Note Tripping Lever Head Forced Down by Piston

SINGLE SHOT FIRE

Bren Gun— Fire Selector

of the immensity of the task can be gained from the fact that there were 270 operations on the body alone[1] and for this 550 gauges were required each made to an accuracy of 0·0005in. The gun was made by conventional milling from the solid and the first gun was finished in September 1937. This was a very creditable performance indeed. By December 1937 42 guns were completed and by July 1938 production was 300 a week—rising to 400 a week in September 1939.

By June 1940 more than 30,000 guns had been produced and issued.

The gun was only manufactured at Enfield and one air raid would have been absolutely catastrophic in its effect. Magazines were manufactured by BSA and the Austin Motor Works. These gave trouble because they would only function with 29 rounds instead of 30. This was found to be a drawing error in the conversion from the rimless 7·92mm cartridge design.

After Dunkirk only about 2300 Bren guns remained in England[2] and Enfield worked flat out to produce more. By 1943 production at Enfield had reached 1000 guns a week. Production was started in 1940 by John Inglis in Canada and by the Lithgow Small Arms Factory in Australia which produced 150 guns a week by 1942. Inglis also manufactured the gun in 7·92mm for China. In 1952 the Inglis version of the Mk II Bren was manufactured in Formosa as the M41 in ·30-06.

The original gun was designated the Mk I. The Mk II gun had the same length barrel, a simplified rear sight, and the flash hider—gas regulator—front sight which was originally a single stainless steel fabrication was produced as three separate units with only the regulator in stainless steel. The bipod was made with non telescopic legs and the handle below the butt was omitted. These changes to assist production increased the weight from 22lb 2oz to 23lb 3oz. The Mk III simplified

---

[1]'Pictorial History of the Machine Gun' published by Ian Allan Ltd. [2]International Armament—Johnson & Lockhoven.

production, reduced barrel length, and also the gun weight was reduced to 19lb 5oz. The Mk IV had the shorter barrel and weight was reduced to the minimum compatible with the stresses imposed by the ·303 Mk VII cartridge.

The differences can be summarized as:

	Barrel length (in)	Overall length (in)	Weight
Mk I	25	45·5	22lb 2oz
Mk II	25	45·5	23lb 3oz
Mk III	22·25	42·9	19lb 5oz
Mk IV	22·25	42·9	19lb 2oz

The L4 Bren Series

When the decision was made to adopt the 7·62mm NATO round various conversions of the ·303 Bren gun were made to adapt them for 7·62mm. These generally employed the breech block made for the Canadian 7·92mm guns with new barrels.

A brief summary of the L4 series follows:

L4A1 Converted Mk III ·303 Bren. First known as the X10E1. Two steel barrels. Bipod Mk I. Now obsolescent.

L4A2 Converted Mk III ·303 Bren. First known as the X10E2. Two steel barrels. Light bipod. Land and Naval use. Now obsolescent.

L4A3 Converted Mk II ·303 Bren. One chromium plated barrel. Now obsolescent for land service.

L4A4 Converted Mk III ·303 Bren. One chromium plated barrel. Current weapon all services.

L4A5 Converted Mk II ·303 Bren. Two steel barrels. Obsolescent for Land and Air Service. Still in Naval service.

L4A6 Converted L4A1. One chrome plated barrel. Introduced only for land service. Now obsolescent.

L4A7 Conversion of Mk I ·303 Bren. None made but drawings prepared for an overseas buyer.

Operation of the Bren Gun

The Bren Light Machine Gun is a magazine fed, gas operated gun using a tilting block locking system lifting the rear end of the breech block into a locking recess in the top of the body.

During the period of initial pressure build up the body, barrel, breech block, gas cylinder and bipod recoil on the butt slide approximately $\frac{1}{4}$in. The movement is buffered by the piston buffer and spring. When this energy has been absorbed the piston buffer spring reasserts itself and returns the body, barrel, cylinder and bipod to their normal positions on the butt slide. This recoil and run out of these assemblies reduces the shock experienced by the firer and makes for less breakages in the affected components.

When the gun is fired the gases force the bullet up the bore and a small proportion of them is diverted through a tapping in the barrel, passes through the regulator and impinges on the piston head. The piston is driven back. Attached to the piston by a flexible joint is the piston extension on which is supported the breech block.

A piston post on the extension fits into the hollow

Bren Gun Mk 2. Barrel is Mk 1. Note back sight. No shoulder strap. No AA handle. No adjustment to bipod leg length   (*Pattern Room RSAF, Enfield*)

Bren Mk 2/1. Barrel is Mk 2
(*Pattern Room RSAF, Enfield*)

Bren Mk 2/1. Flash hider, sights and regulator now separate components. Only gas block in stainless steel. Note flat gas shield. (*Pattern Room RSAF, Enfield*)

Bren Mk 3
(*Pattern Room RSAF, Enfield*)

Bren 7·92mm manufactured in Canada by Inglis for China   (*Pattern Room RSAF, Enfield*)

Marking on 7·92mm Bren supplied to China

(*Pattern Room RSAF, Enfield*)

Bren Mk 2 ·303in by Inglis converted to
·280 to take the 7mm Mk 1Z round produced for the EM2 rifle
(*Pattern Room, RSAF Enfield*)

Close up of lettering on ·280 conversion

(*Pattern Room RSAF, Enfield*)

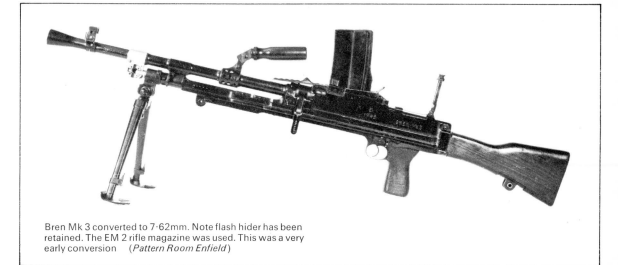

Bren Mk 3 converted to 7·62mm. Note flash hider has been
retained. The EM 2 rifle magazine was used. This was a very
early conversion   (*Pattern Room Enfield*)

interior of the breech block and two ramps hold the rear of the block up into the locked position engaged in the locking recess at the top of the body.

When the piston extension moves back there is a movement of about $1\frac{1}{4}$ in during which the bolt remains fully locked. Further movement removes the ramp support under the block and then an inclined surface on the rear of the piston post forces the back end of the bolt down and unlocking is completed. The tilting motion of the breech block provides primary extraction and the cartridge case is first unseated in the chamber and then withdrawn by the extractor claw as the breech block moves back. A

Close up of lettering on converted Mk 3 Bren
(*Pattern Room RSAF, Enfield*)

Bren Mk 3 conversion to 7·62mm. Note modified EM 2 rifle magazine
(*Pattern Room RSAF, Enfield*)

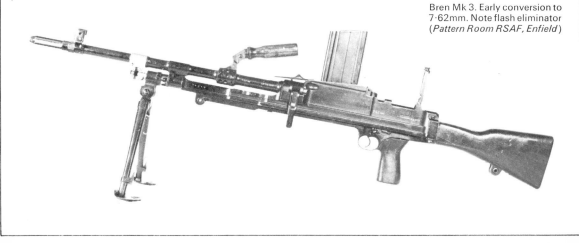

Bren Mk 3. Early conversion to 7·62mm. Note flash eliminator
(*Pattern Room RSAF, Enfield*)

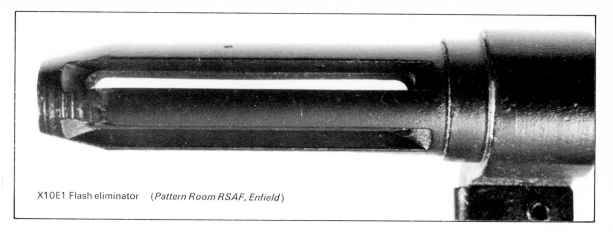

X10E1 Flash eliminator   (*Pattern Room RSAF, Enfield*)

fully fixed ejector rides in a groove on top of the block and it is chisel shaped so that as it strikes the brass of the cartridge case above the primer cap, brass is burred over the cap to prevent the latter falling out and causing a stoppage. The empty case is pushed through a cut-away section in the piston extension and thrown downwards out of the gun. As the piston goes back the return spring is compressed, storing energy, and this plus the action of the soft buffer throws the piston forward again. The soft buffer has a low coefficient of restitution and so the piston speed forward is not excessive and this keeps the cyclic rate to about 500 rounds a minute. The feed horns on top of the front of the block push a round out of the 30 round box magazine mounted vertically above the gun and the bullet is guided downwards into the chamber. As the cartridge goes forward the extractor claw clips over the rim of the round. When the round is fully

chambered bolt movement ceases. The piston continues forward under its own momentum, and the remaining force in the return spring, and the two ramps at the rear end lift the rear of the breech block so that the locking surface on top of the rear of the block rises into the locking recess in the body. The ramps remain under the block and hold it locked. The forward movement of the piston continues for another $1\frac{1}{4}$in and the front face of the piston post acts as a hammer to drive the spring retracted firing pin into the cap at the base of the cartridge.

It can be seen from the accompanying diagram that the system is extremely simple. It has one mechanical imperfection in that the locking ramps at the rear of the piston extension are attempting to lift the rear of the breech block against the top of the gun body throughout the forward stroke. This increases the friction force and it is noteworthy that in later guns of Czech manufacture such as the

Close up of lettering on Mk 3 conversion to 7·62mm X10E1

(*Pattern Room RSAF, Enfield*)

Bren Mk 3 conversion to 7·62mm X10E1. This was the first of the experimental X10 series
(*Pattern Room RSAF, Enfield*)

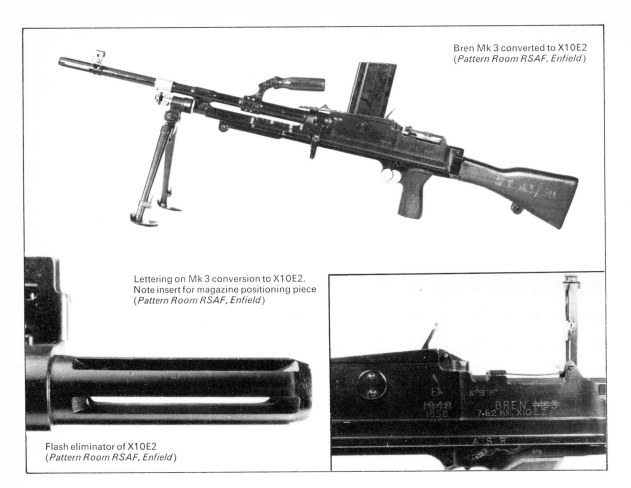

Bren Mk 3 converted to X10E2
(*Pattern Room RSAF, Enfield*)

Lettering on Mk 3 conversion to X10E2.
Note insert for magazine positioning piece
(*Pattern Room RSAF, Enfield*)

Flash eliminator of X10E2
(*Pattern Room RSAF, Enfield*)

Zb 53—BESA—and Vz 52 these ramps have been made with a vertical leading edge and the initial bolt raising is produced by cams in the sides of the hollow block. Mechanical safety on the gun is provided before firing by the initial non-alignment of the cartridge and the firing pin in the bolt and subsequently by the free movement of the piston post of $1\frac{1}{4}$in after locking is completed before it contacts the firing pin. Mechanical safety after firing comes from:

a The location of the gas vent which is 15in from the breech face.

b The free travel of $1\frac{1}{4}$in of the piston post before the inclined ramp starts to pull the block down out of the locked position.

It is interesting to note that in 1933 when 'caps out' was first observed in the ZGB 32 it was considered to be due to excess residual pressure caused by unduly early unlocking. A series of electrical contacts was set up in the gun and it was found that the bullet was 2·2ft from the muzzle when unlocking began and 13·2ft from the muzzle when unlocking was complete. Nevertheless the free travel of the piston was increased in the ZGB 33.

The applied safety disconnects the trigger from the sear by holding the trigger lever in the middle of the sear window.

In theory this is not a satisfactory arrangement as a heavy jar caused by dropping the gun could dislodge the sear from the piston bent. In practice there is no record that this has ever happened.

The gas regulator was installed in the Bren gun—it was not in the early Zb series—to give greater flexibility when the gun is firing under adverse conditions produced by sandy terrain, mud, firing at elevation or depression. The regulator has four tracks and a larger diameter gas track can be rotated into position as required. It should be noted that the gas impulse is only applied for a very short distance and then the gas escapes to atmosphere through vents bored in the cylinder walls. If excessive fouling occurs the bipod can be twisted and this cuts away any build up of carbon which is then dispersed by the next blast of gas. This feature produces an extremely reliable gun even after prolonged firing.

The barrel can be changed in a matter of seconds by raising the barrel latch and pulling the barrel forward using the carrying handle. With the gun fired at 120 rounds—four magazines—a minute, the barrel requires changing every $2\frac{1}{2}$ minutes. The hot barrel can be cooled by air after removal from the gun or as often happened in action by laying it in wet grass or even in a stream.

The weapon can be fired either at full automatic or at single shot. The latter facility is employed to conserve ammunition, prolong barrel life and for tactical deception. The selector mechanism is illustrated. The sear has a window through which projects the tripping lever. When the change lever is rotated to 'single shot' the tripping lever bears against the upper surface of the window in the sear

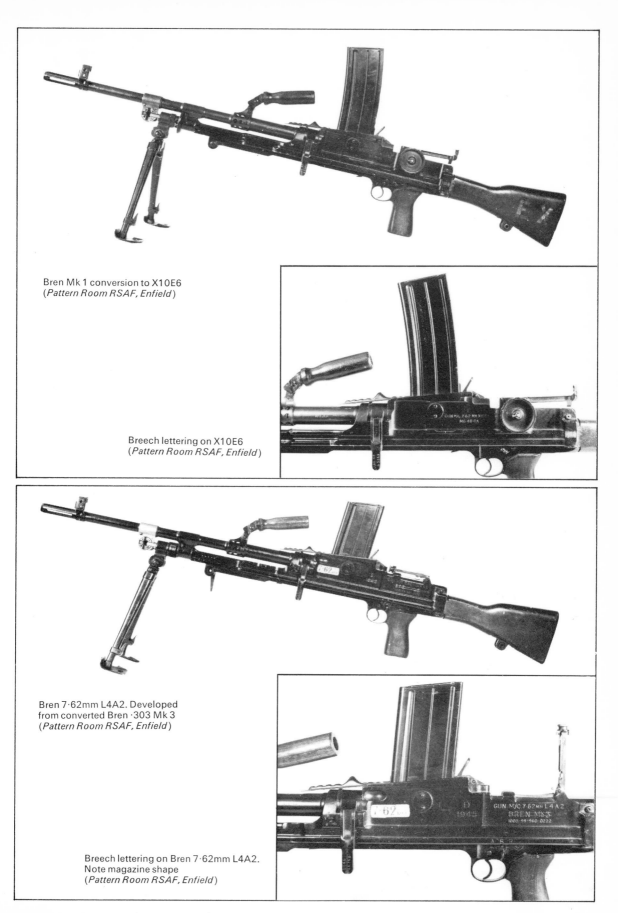

Bren Mk 1 conversion to X10E6
(*Pattern Room RSAF, Enfield*)

Breech lettering on X10E6
(*Pattern Room RSAF, Enfield*)

Bren 7·62mm L4A2. Developed
from converted Bren ·303 Mk 3
(*Pattern Room RSAF, Enfield*)

Breech lettering on Bren 7·62mm L4A2.
Note magazine shape
(*Pattern Room RSAF, Enfield*)

and its tripping head is raised into the path of the gas piston which depresses the tripping head as it comes forward. This forces the tripping lever down away from the sear window and the sear is released to rise and hold the piston to the rear. Releasing the trigger re-positions the tripping lever against the top surface of the sear window and operating the trigger fires one more shot.

When the change lever is set to 'auto' the tripping lever is forced down to bear on the bottom side of the sear window and the tripping lever head is pulled down clear of the piston. The gun continues firing as long as ammunition remains in the magazine and the trigger is depressed.

The gun is usually employed as a light machine gun using a bipod but during the war a tripod was available. This enabled the gun to fire on fixed lines and could also be adapted readily for anti-aircraft use.

The 30 round box magazine was universal but had to be loaded with care as overlapping rims could cause a stoppage. A 100 round high speed drum magazine was produced for anti aircraft fire early in World War II but was not widely used because it was heavy, difficult to load quickly and also awkward to carry.

The Mk I gun had a tangent drum back sight but to simplify production a vertical leaf backsight was installed on subsequent marks.

The Mk I gun also had a handle under the butt for a left hand grip and a strap on the butt plate to rest over the shoulder. Both these features were abandoned for later marks.

Bren ·303 Mk 1 on Mottley mounting for AA use
(*Pattern Room RSAF, Enfield*)

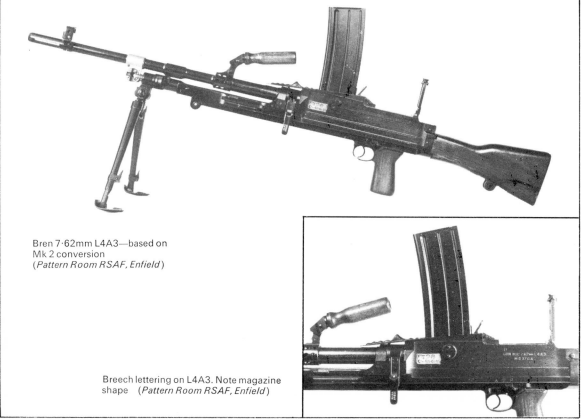

Bren 7·62mm L4A3—based on Mk 2 conversion
(*Pattern Room RSAF, Enfield*)

Breech lettering on L4A3. Note magazine shape   (*Pattern Room RSAF, Enfield*)

War time experimental reversible barrel
Bren. The barrel had a chamber at each end
and could be reversed when worn
(*Pattern Room RSAF, Enfield*)

Mk 1 Bren converted to 7·92mm at
Enfield in 1938. Enfield hoped that the
7·92mm cartridge then being adopted for
the BESA could become standard for all
machine guns
(*Pattern Room RSAF, Enfield*)

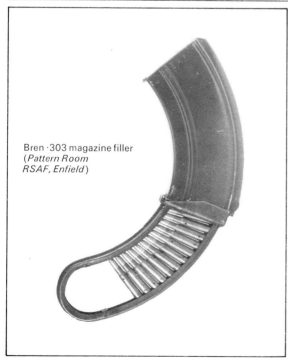

Bren ·303 magazine filler
(*Pattern Room
RSAF, Enfield*)

Stripping

The Bren gun is one of the easiest there is to strip.
After removing the magazine and ensuring the
chamber is empty :

a Remove the barrel.
b Push the body locking pin from left to right.
c Pull back the butt and trigger group.
d Pull back the cocking handle and remove the
piston and breech block.

Re-assemble in reverse order.

Conclusion

The Bren gun was the standard light machine gun
of all British and British Empire Troops. It was used
by the Chinese against the Japanese and by French,
Dutch and Belgian resistance groups. It saw action
in every theatre of war. It was simple, reliable and
accurate.

It had the confidence and affection of all who used it
and many soldiers today prefer it in its present
7·62mm form to the heavier belt fed L7A2 GPMG
in the section role. In Malaya, Borneo, Radfan and
in Aden it added to its laurels and is regarded by
many as the finest LMG ever in service with any
army.

High speed 200 AA magazine for
·303 Bren. This was not popular and fell
speedily into disuse
(*Pattern Room RSAF, Enfield*)

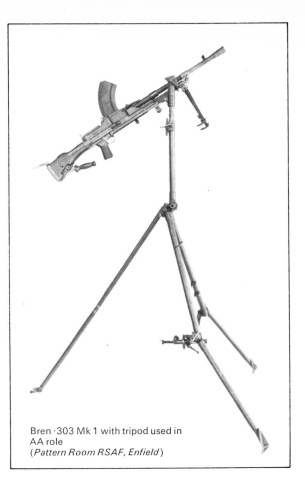

Bren ·303 Mk 1 with tripod used in
AA role
(*Pattern Room RSAF, Enfield*)

DATA BREN LMG ·303

Small Arms Editor: A. J. R. Cormack

	Mk I	Mk II	Mk III	Mk IV
Weight	22lb 2oz	23lb 3oz	19lb 5oz	19lb 2oz
Length (in)	45·5	45·5	42·9	42·9
Barrel length (in)	25·0	25·0	22·25	22·25
Barrel weight	6lb 4$\frac{1}{4}$oz	6lb 7$\frac{1}{2}$oz	5lb 1$\frac{1}{2}$oz	5lb
No of grooves	6	6	6	6
Type of rifling	Enfield	Enfield	Enfield	Enfield
Twist	Right hand	Right hand	Right hand	Right hand
Pitch	1 turn in 10"	1 turn in 10"	1 turn in 10"	1 turn in 10"
Diameter of bore (in)	H0·304	H0·304	H0·304	H0·304
	L0·301	L0·301	L0·301	L0·301
Width of groove (in)	0·088	0·088	0·088	0·088
Depth of groove (in)	0·0057	0·0057	0·0057	0·0057
Sight radius (in)	31·02	30·80	27·31	27·31
Cartridge	·303 Mk VII			
Bullet weight (gr)	174			
Charge weight (gr)	37			
Muzzle velocity (ft/s)	2440			
Muzzle energy (ft lbf)	2300			
Muzzle momentum $\frac{\text{(lb ft)}}{\text{s}}$	81			
Recoil energy (ft lbf)	6			
Range—max effective (yards)	1000			
max (yards)	3300			
Magazine capacity	30			
Weight empty	1lb 1oz			
Weight full	2lb 12oz			

ERMA SUBMACHINE GUNS

A. J. R. Cormack

Erma Submachine guns in action during World War II   (*IWM*)

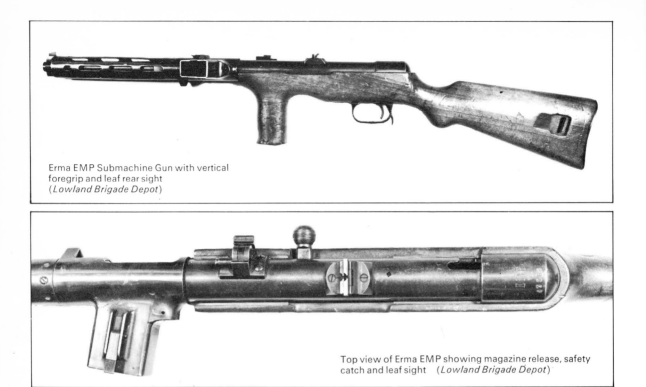

Erma EMP Submachine Gun with vertical
foregrip and leaf rear sight
(*Lowland Brigade Depot*)

Top view of Erma EMP showing magazine release, safety
catch and leaf sight   (*Lowland Brigade Depot*)

The receiver mounted safety catch shown at fire and the leaf
sight with the 100 metre blade raised
(*Lowland Brigade Depot*)

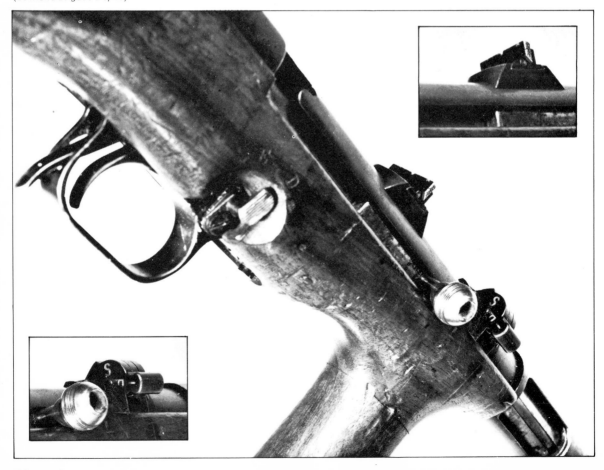

If any firm has exhibited the continued development of a weapon type it is the firm of Erma. They have developed the MP (Machinen-Pistole) series of submachine guns for over 40 years and as a result the weapon range displays the advances in material and in technique of manufacture which have taken place.

Erma, ERfurt MAchinen = ERMA, was founded in 1924 by Berthold Geiupel, who had been the Director of the main arsenal at Erfurt which had been disbanded after World War I in 1919.

Although the first submachine guns had been demonstrated in prototype form during the first World War, it was not until 1927 that an efficient weapon was developed. Once again, as with many weapons of this era, the early submachine gun developments were put to their initial tests during the Spanish Civil War.

Vollmer

First of the Erma produced submachine guns was designed by Heinrich Vollmer in collaboration with Berthold Geipel. This weapon was patented in 1927 and in 1928 production was started by Erma Werke in Erfurt at the Erfurt Machine Works. The submachine gun was produced in two versions; one with a telescopic monopod and a long tapering barrel, and the second without the monopod and a shorter barrel. These weapons were sold in the 1920s in France, Mexico and a number of South American countries as well as being used in limited quantities in the Spanish Civil War. Both the Vollmer and its derivation the Erma EMP fire from an open bolt and both utilise a telescoping main operating spring which was to remain a feature of many later models. The telescoping operating spring is an arrangement whereby the spring is guided by a tube which telescopes on recoil, thus protecting the spring and preventing it from being disorted.

EMP

One of the differences between the EMP and the earlier weapon, and certainly the most noticeable, was the addition of a barrel jacket. The EMP was produced in three different versions. First, the Model 1935 had a tangent rear sight, a long barrel with a barrel jacket and a fitting for a bayonet. It is possible that it was sold to Yugoslavia in the mid-thirties. The second model which was produced in two slightly different forms was mechanically the same and only differed in the stock and fore-end. The third model, of which the largest number was produced, had its main use during the Spanish Civil War. The difference between it and the two previous models was the use of a different safety device. All these models of the EMP use the basic Vollmer action.

MP38

During the 1930s the German armoured forces requested a light, burst fire weapon. However, the German Army High Command feeling that there was no need for a weapon of this type placed no contracts. Erma however continued with the development of prototypes based on the Vollmer design using the telescoping main spring behind the bolt as on the original weapons. In 1938 the weapon in its final prototype form was sold to the German Border Police and to a number of countries, in small batches.

In 1938, with a change of mind which typifies the problems facing a firm dealing with Government Departments, the German Army High Command summoned the Director and owner of the Erma Factory, Berthold Giepel, and ordered him to design and manufacture a weapon which would fill the need of the armoured vehicle crews and paratroops. It was providential that Erma had continued with the development of submachine guns as the order was

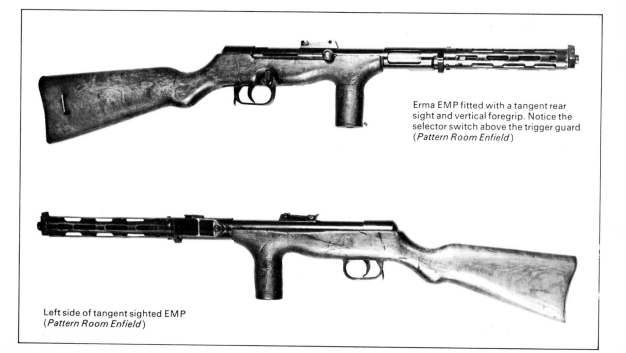

Erma EMP fitted with a tangent rear sight and vertical foregrip. Notice the selector switch above the trigger guard (*Pattern Room Enfield*)

Left side of tangent sighted EMP (*Pattern Room Enfield*)

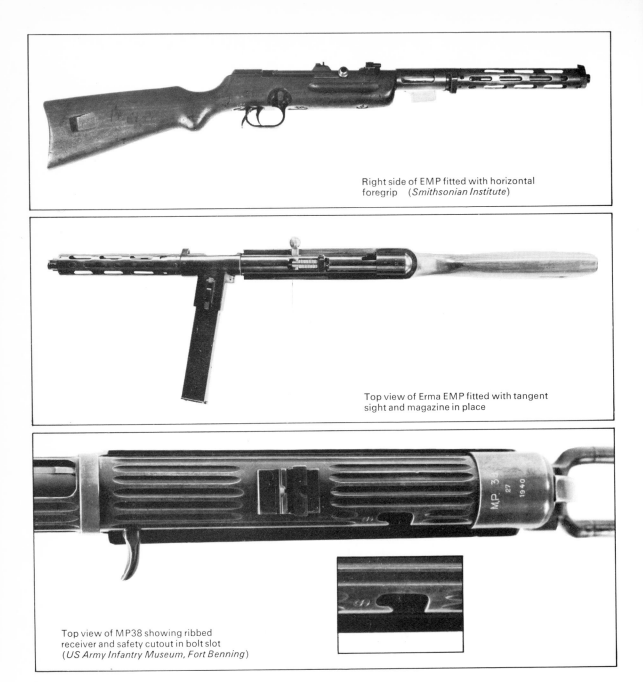

Right side of EMP fitted with horizontal foregrip   (*Smithsonian Institute*)

Top view of Erma EMP fitted with tangent sight and magazine in place

Top view of MP38 showing ribbed receiver and safety cutout in bolt slot (*US Army Infantry Museum, Fort Benning*)

to be carried out immediately. Erma named their new weapon the MP38. The MP38 is the fore-runner of the most modern types of submachine gun in that it pioneers the use of plastics as a substitute for wood, incorporates a folding shoulder stock and is easy to manufacture. The weapon fires from an open bolt and uses the telescoping main operating spring, the receiver is made from steel tube and the grips and fore-end from plastic. The grip frame is an aluminium casting. A very popular misconception which must be corrected is that the weapon was designed by Hugo Smeisser. This is incorrect and can only be attributed to the fact that Smeisser worked for the Heinel firm as General Manager. This firm, under the management of Smeisser, produced the MP38, and when the MP40 was produced they not only produced it but also a modi-

fication—the MP41. Erma state very forcibly in correspondence with the author their claim to the design and their justifiable concern over the mistake. All Erma produced MP38s have the Erma codes ayf 27 and were produced at the Erma plant at Erfurt during the years 1938 to 1940. The MP38 was superior to any weapon used at that time by the Allies when ease of production and combat effectiveness are considered. The Allied Combat Troops coveted it, admired it and feared it.

MP38/40

The only serious problem encountered with the MP38 and one encountered even with modern sub-machine guns was that of safety. The problem is that, with an open bolt firing gun, when the bolt is

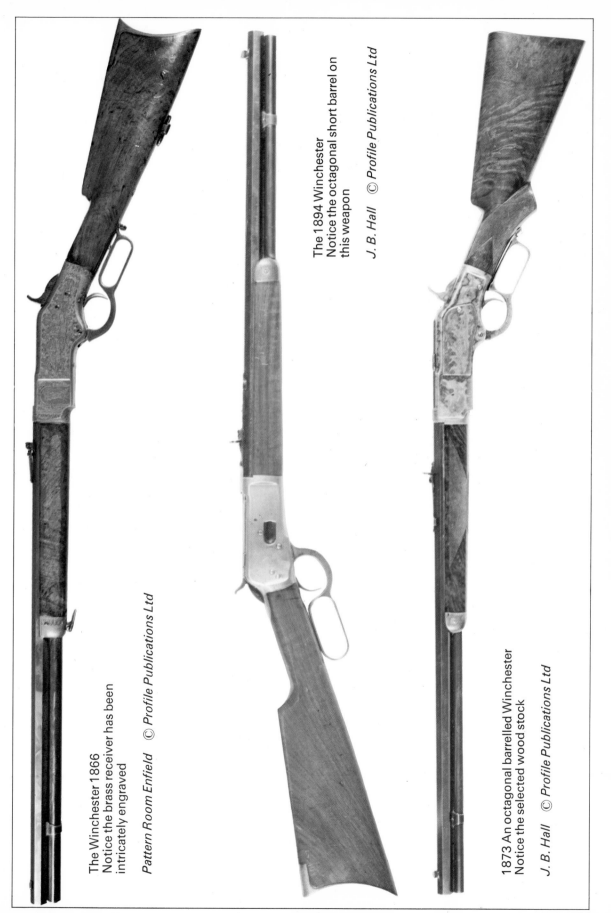

The Winchester 1866
Notice the brass receiver has been intricately engraved

Pattern Room Enfield © *Profile Publications Ltd*

The 1894 Winchester
Notice the octagonal short barrel on this weapon

J. B. Hall © *Profile Publications Ltd*

1873 An octagonal barrelled Winchester
Notice the selected wood stock

J. B. Hall © *Profile Publications Ltd*

The right side of the MK1 Bren
manufactured in 1943 at Enfield

Lowland Brigade Depot

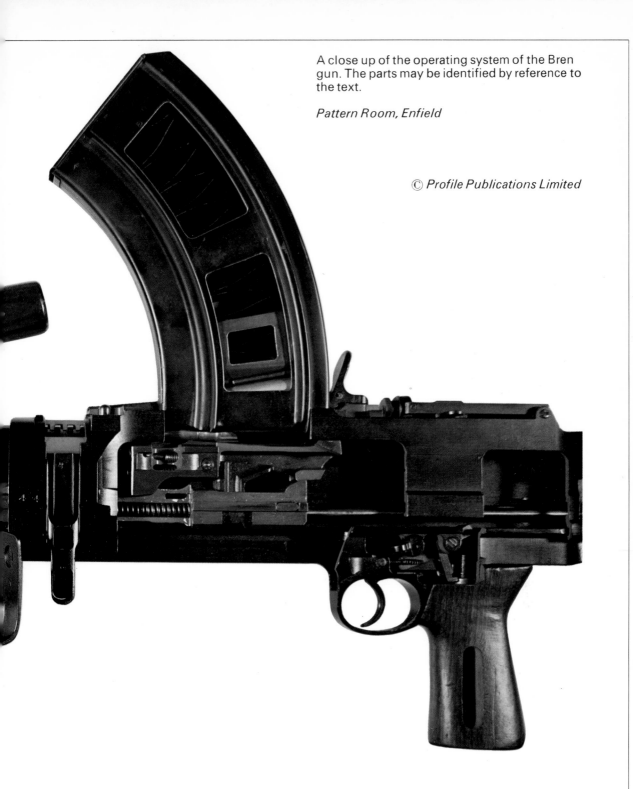

A close up of the operating system of the Bren gun. The parts may be identified by reference to the text.

Pattern Room, Enfield

© *Profile Publications Limited*

Notice the 30-round magazine, magazine cover and rear sight.

Lowland Brigade Depot

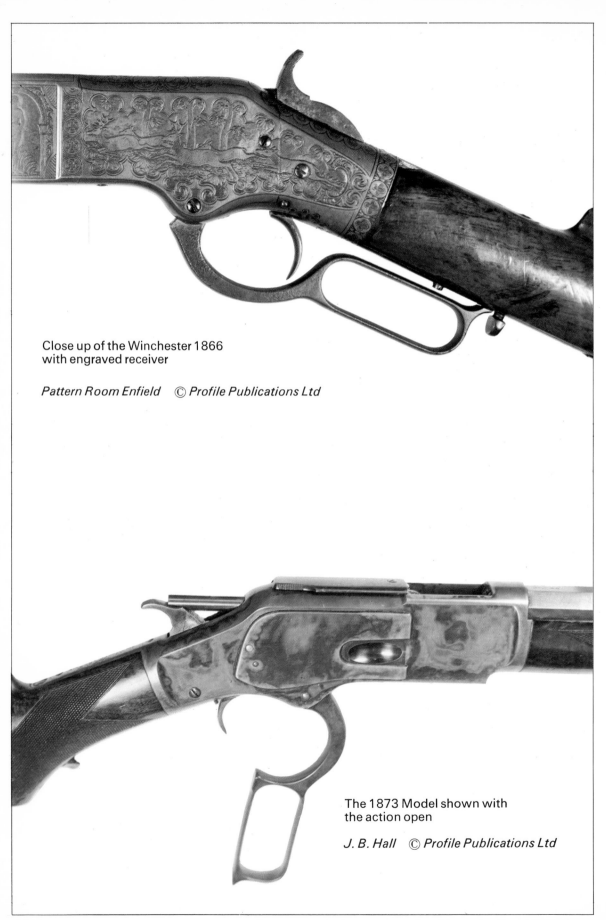

Close up of the Winchester 1866
with engraved receiver

Pattern Room Enfield   © Profile Publications Ltd

The 1873 Model shown with
the action open

J. B. Hall   © Profile Publications Ltd

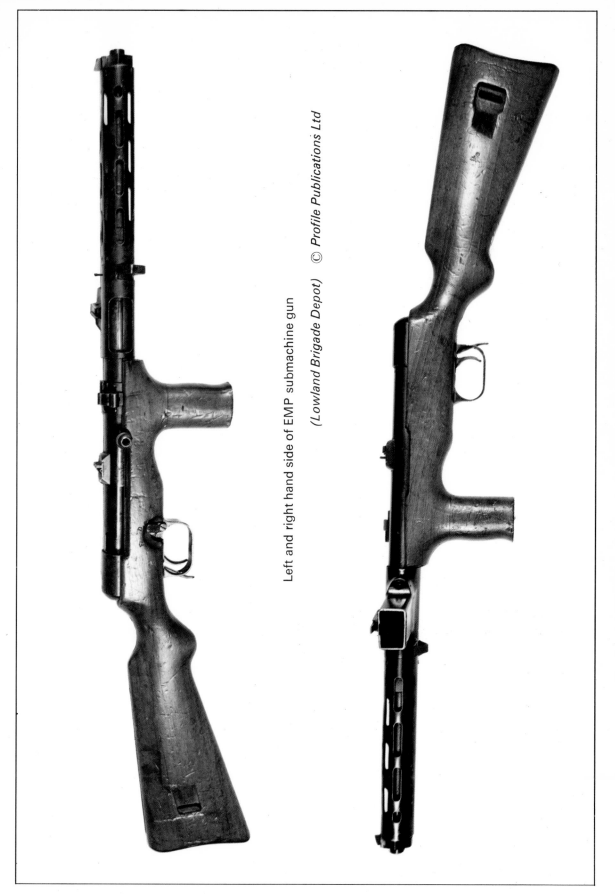

Left and right hand side of EMP submachine gun

(Lowland Brigade Depot) © *Profile Publications Ltd*

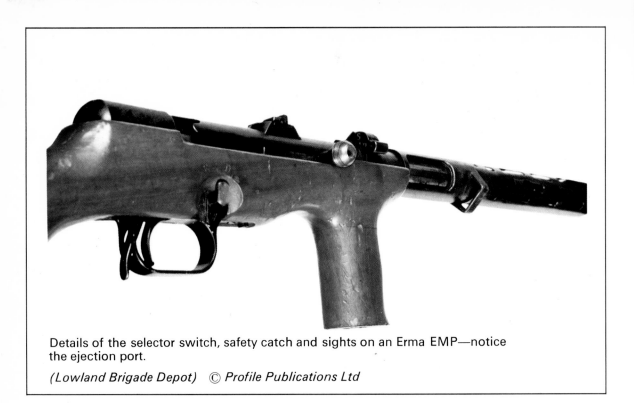

Details of the selector switch, safety catch and sights on an Erma EMP—notice
the ejection port.

(Lowland Brigade Depot) © *Profile Publications Ltd*

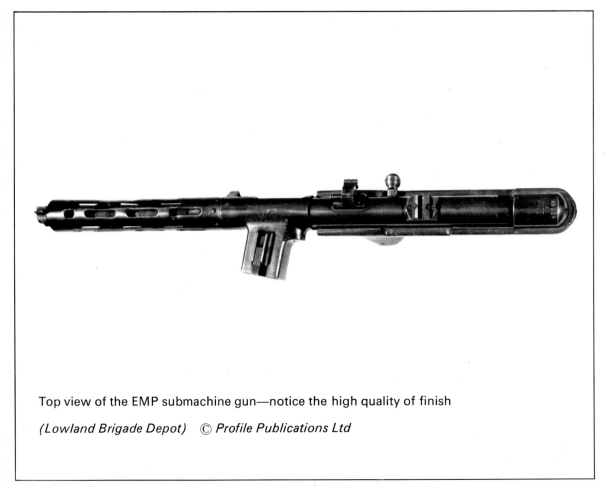

Top view of the EMP submachine gun—notice the high quality of finish

(Lowland Brigade Depot) © *Profile Publications Ltd*

Model 1921 Thompson with box magazine fitted
Lyman sights raised and a 50-round drum magazine

Lowland Brigade Depot © *Profile Publications Ltd*

Top view of a Model 1921 showing the actuator knob and the Lyman rear sight

Lowland Brigade Depot © *Profile Publications Ltd*

A field stripped Model 1921. The trigger mechanism not stripped as this is a workshop job

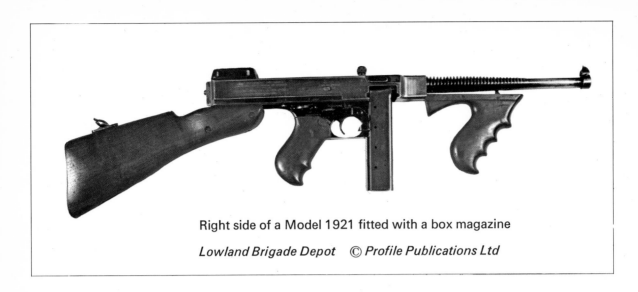

Right side of a Model 1921 fitted with a box magazine

Lowland Brigade Depot © *Profile Publications Ltd*

Model 1928 Thompson fitted with
box magazine and Cutts compensator

Lowland Brigade Depot © *Profile Publications Ltd*

The bolt from a Model 1921 showing the angled slot and above the 'H' piece

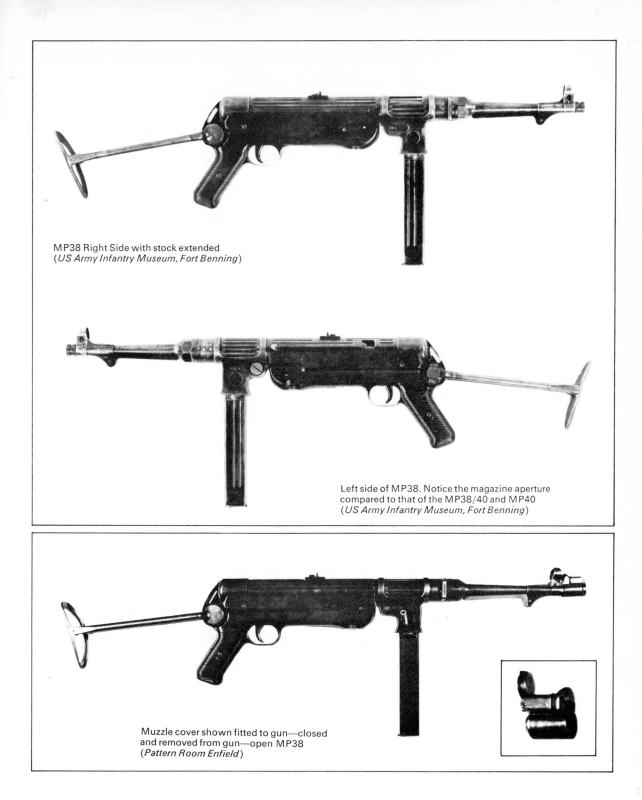

MP38 Right Side with stock extended
(*US Army Infantry Museum, Fort Benning*)

Left side of MP38. Notice the magazine aperture
compared to that of the MP38/40 and MP40
(*US Army Infantry Museum, Fort Benning*)

Muzzle cover shown fitted to gun—closed
and removed from gun—open MP38
(*Pattern Room Enfield*)

jarred out of the sear, it goes forward and fires the
gun. This was cured by fitting a positive bolt lock in
the form of a lock on the bolt handle which fitted
into a notch in the receiver. This was such a simple
modification that many MP38s were modified at
the Army Ordnance Workshops with parts supplied
by Erma; it, along with a modified magazine well, is
often given the designation MP38/40. The development from MP38 to 38/40 to MP40 was one of

gradual improvement and thus a number of
modified weapons will not fit any one designation.

MP40
The successor to the MP38/40 was the MP40 which
simplified the manufacture one stage further; the
weapon was constructed of stamped sheet steel
being brazed and spot-welded together. The plastic
fore-grip was moulded from a phenolic resin giving

MP38 in action during World War II. Notice the spare magazine pouch slung from the waist   (*Photo-War*)

Left side of MP38 with stock folded and showing magazine loader

MP38/40. Notice the magazine housing and the magazine loader   (*Pattern Room Enfield*)

Left side of MP38/40 with stock extended and magazine loader fitted to magazine (*Pattern Room Enfield*)

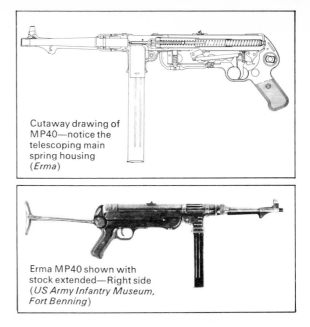

Cutaway drawing of MP40—notice the telescoping main spring housing (*Erma*)

Erma MP40 shown with stock extended—Right side (*US Army Infantry Museum, Fort Benning*)

a high strength combined with a low overall weight and the advantage of insulation in extremes of temperature. Another important point was the use of low carbon steel thus conserving the more-difficult-to-produce alloy steels. This combined with construction using sub-assemblies, and the ability to have these sub-contracted made the MP40 an almost ideal weapon to manufacture under wartime conditions. These techniques have been copied in nearly every major submachine gun since. The MP40 was not only manufactured by Erma but also by Steyr and Heinel, and between 1940 and 1944 there were approximately one million produced. The codes encountered on the MP40s signifying the manufacturer are as follows : 27—pre 1940 Erma : ayf—post 1940. In addition the last two numbers of the date are often added. The Steyr factory in Austria : 660—for 1941 and BNZ for post 1941 production. The Heinel code is fxo : cos for Merz-Werke : knd National Krup Registier. As would be expected in a gun produced under wartime conditions, there were a number of progressive modifications ; the most important of which were a two-piece retracting handle and a ribbed metal stamped magazine housing. The final modification was carried out by Steyr in which the grip frame and the receiver were made as one. A few late date weapons have a fixed firing pin and the telescoping main spring deleted. This was caused by the shortage of materials and an MG42 spring was cut in half and used, with the result that the rate of fire was erratic. To try to increase the magazine capacity there was a modification called the MP40/2 which featured dual magazine housing. This enabled two standard 32-round magazines to be fitted to the gun, one being slid across when the first was empty.

The Americans tested the MP40 at the Aberdeen Proving Ground in 1940/41. The results were that the function and reliability were extremely good and the accuracy excellent. This, from the Aberdeen Proving Ground, is indeed a compliment.

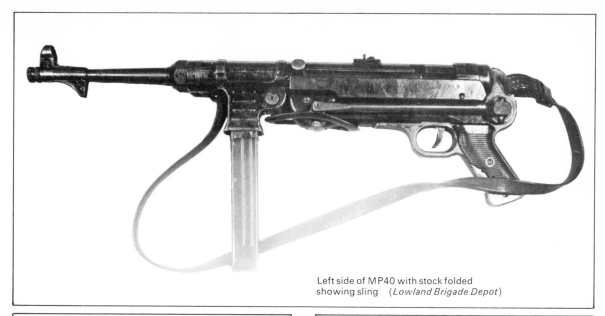

Left side of MP40 with stock folded
showing sling (*Lowland Brigade Depot*)

Top view of MP40 showing leaf rear sight and the bolt safety
slot (*Lowland Brigade Depot*)

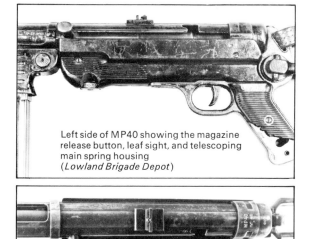

Left side of MP40 showing the magazine
release button, leaf sight, and telescoping
main spring housing
(*Lowland Brigade Depot*)

Top view of MP40 showing the ejector slot, bolt, safety slot
with mark 'S' and the manufacturers code
(*US Army Infantry Museum, Fort Benning*)

Close-up of two piece bolt handle with the safety device in the
firing position (*Lowland Brigade Depot*)

The manufacturers code and markings on MP40
(*Lowland Brigade Depot*)

The production figures for the years 1940-1944 are
as follows : 1940—113700 ; 1941—239300 ; 1942—
231500 ; 1943—234300 ; 1944—228600.

MP41
The previously referred to MP41 which was
developed by Smeisser at the Heinel factory Soaul

used a receiver and action directly copied from the
MP40 but a wooden stock and a fire selector
mechanism similar to the Smeisser designed
MP28/2. This weapon is often marked 'MP41
patent Smeisser' ; this possibly giving rise to the
above-mentioned mistaken use of the name.

EMP44
An interesting weapon developed by Erma during
1942/43 was the EMP44. The actual use of this

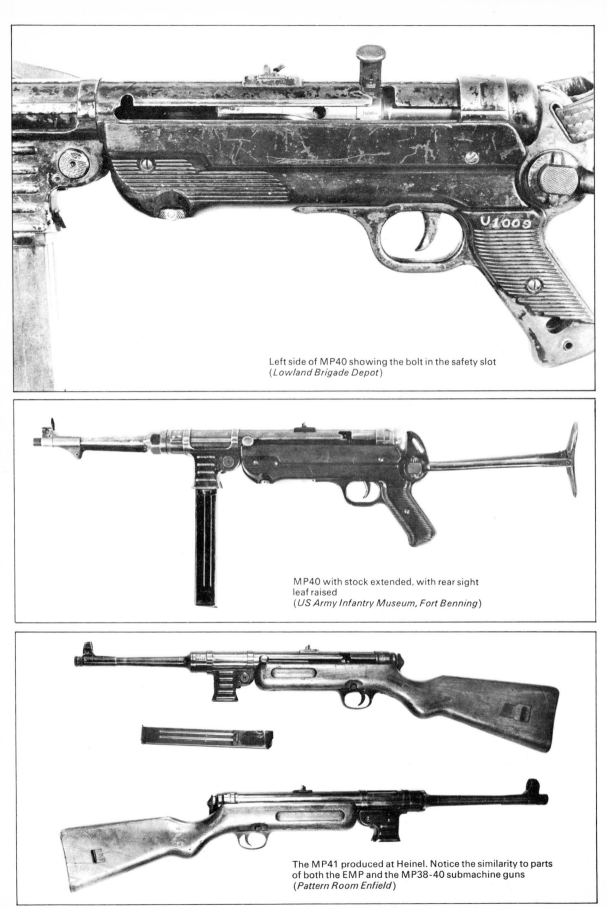

Left side of MP40 showing the bolt in the safety slot
(*Lowland Brigade Depot*)

MP40 with stock extended, with rear sight
leaf raised
(*US Army Infantry Museum, Fort Benning*)

The MP41 produced at Heinel. Notice the similarity to parts
of both the EMP and the MP38-40 submachine guns
(*Pattern Room Enfield*)

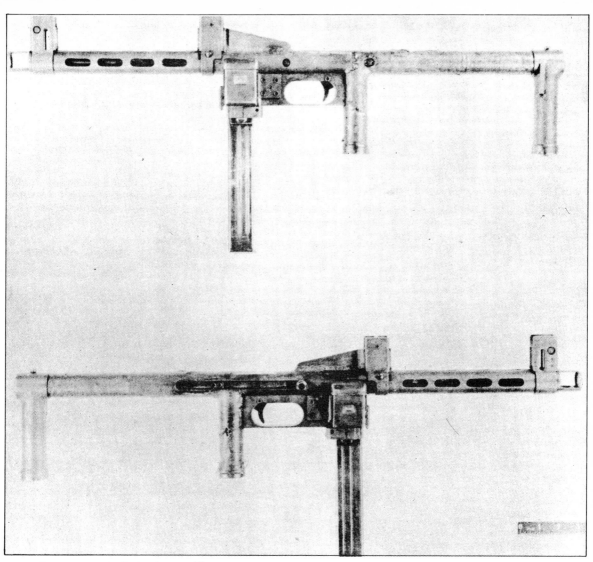

Above: The Erma MP44—Notice the resemblance to
scaffolding and the crude workmanship
(*Aberdeen Proving Ground*)

Below: The MP40 fitted with dual magazine feed
(*Aberdeen Proving Ground*)

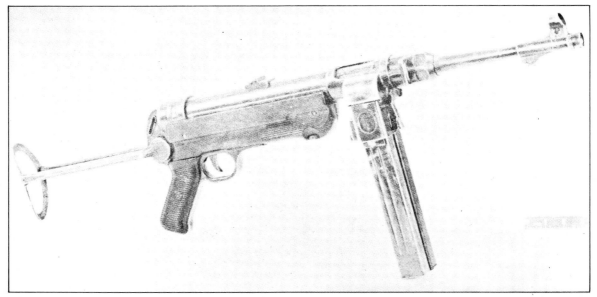

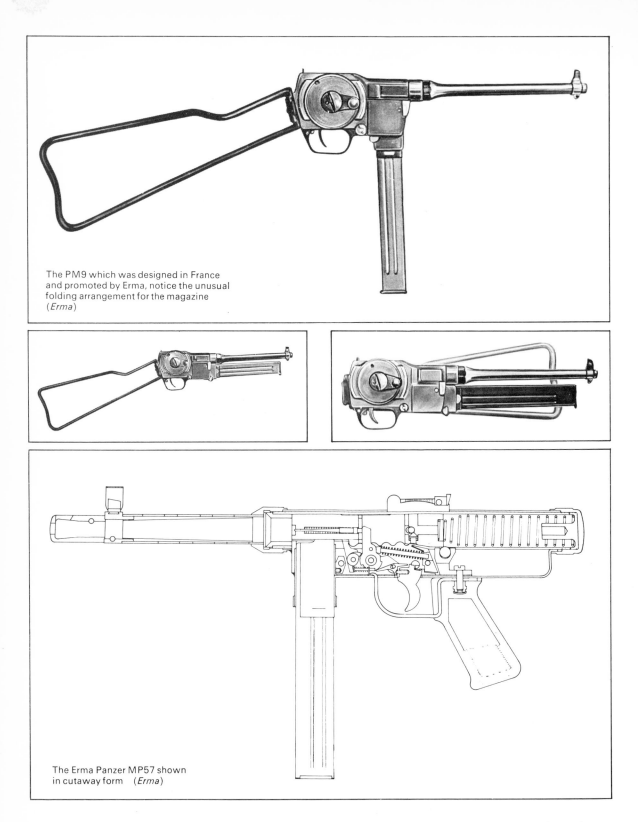

The PM9 which was designed in France and promoted by Erma, notice the unusual folding arrangement for the magazine (*Erma*)

The Erma Panzer MP57 shown in cutaway form   (*Erma*)

weapon has always been in doubt. The pistol grip has a socket which could be used on a mount which would indicate the use from a strong point of a vehicle. Its looks remind one of a conglomeration of scaffolding ! This is very near the truth as all parts including the stock and pistol grip are made from tube and the remainder of the gun from stampings,

the whole gun being rivetted and welded together. The Steyr dual magazine fitting from the MP40 is used with standard MP40 magazines.

POST WAR
After the war most of the personnel of the Erma Werke fled from the Russian occupation and

54

relocated themselves in Bavaria. On 1 January 1951 Erma Werke once more became an arms manufacturing firm. They took up as many of their wartime contracts as possible and as soon as it was permitted they began the design of submachine guns.

PM9

This promotion began in 1955 when a French submachine gun attracted the attention of Erma Werke. This was of particular interest to them as it embodied principles that they were interested in, one of which was a very large variation in the rate of fire. This weapon was designed by Luis Bonnet de Camille.

MP56

In 1956 four prototype MP56 submachine guns designed by Camille were manufactured. However, when the weapons had been built it was felt that it was not yet a production possibility. In the meantime the promoter of the weapon took the contract from Erma and offered it to Mauser where it was to become the Mauser Model 57 submachine gun.

SMART MP57

In 1958 Erma Werke in conjunction with another firm designed an interesting submachine gun, which Erma designated the Erma Panzer MP57. Although not a commercial success it had one extremely interesting feature, that was its ability to fire an anti-tank grenade. To enable the grenade to be fired it had to operate from a closed bolt position (the alternative is to provide a special bolt position for the launcher as the grenade is projected by the gas

pressure and thus the bolt must not blow back or the pressure would not be maintained). Unfortunately the Bundeswehr expressed no interest in the weapon and instead demanded a simple cheap submachine gun to cost as little as £8.

MP58

This weapon was developed in close co-operation with the Federal Ministry of Defence and in the spring of 1959 test models of the MP58 were offered. The MP58 was a neat compact and extremely efficient submachine gun, being insensitive to both dirt and sand. It used the concept of the same sheet metal stampings and telescoping main operating spring as used in the earlier Erma submachine guns and incorporated a neat folding stock. Although it had been developed so closely to the layout desired by the Bundeswehr it was not accepted.

MP59

Erma then developed and announced the MP59 which was merely a logical development of the MP58. It was found however that during tests the requirements of the authorities had once more changed. The people who had set the standards originally and during the development, were no longer in military service and as a result the demands were not only subject to change but some were even contrary to those set out during the development. One feature which was incorporated was a hydraulic buffer to control and slow the rate of fire thus enabling the weapon to have a cyclic rate of fire between 100 and 600 rpm. This was a partial success but as the seals exhibited a tendency to

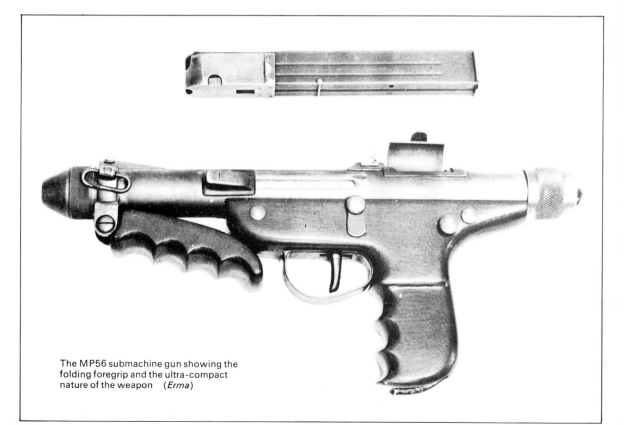

The MP56 submachine gun showing the folding foregrip and the ultra-compact nature of the weapon   (*Erma*)

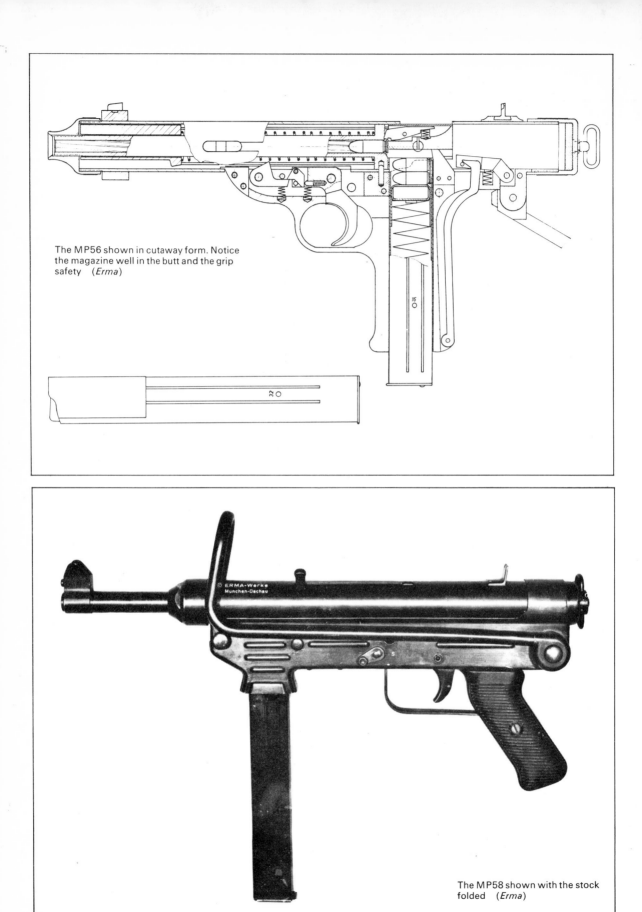

The MP56 shown in cutaway form. Notice the magazine well in the butt and the grip safety   (*Erma*)

The MP58 shown with the stock folded   (*Erma*)

The MP58 left side with stock extended for firing
(*Erma*)

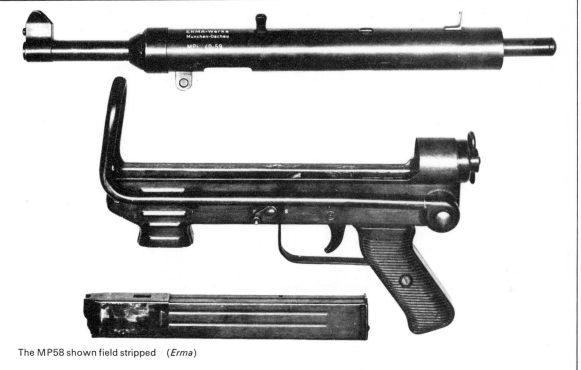

The MP58 shown field stripped   (*Erma*)

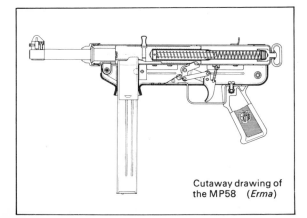

Cutaway drawing of
the MP58   (*Erma*)

wear, the idea was dropped. Erma feel however that
the basic idea has great possibilities and expect that
it will have future applications. The other main
differences between the MP58 and the MP59 are
the substitution of a sliding stock for the collapsible
type, a longer barrel (230mm as opposed to 160mm)
and a different sight.

MP60

With a tenacity which can only be admired, Erma
started the development of a new model in the
spring of 1960. This weapon which used all the
earlier experience was to be the ultimate in safety,
reliability of function and convenience in use, as well
as having a rational and economic production

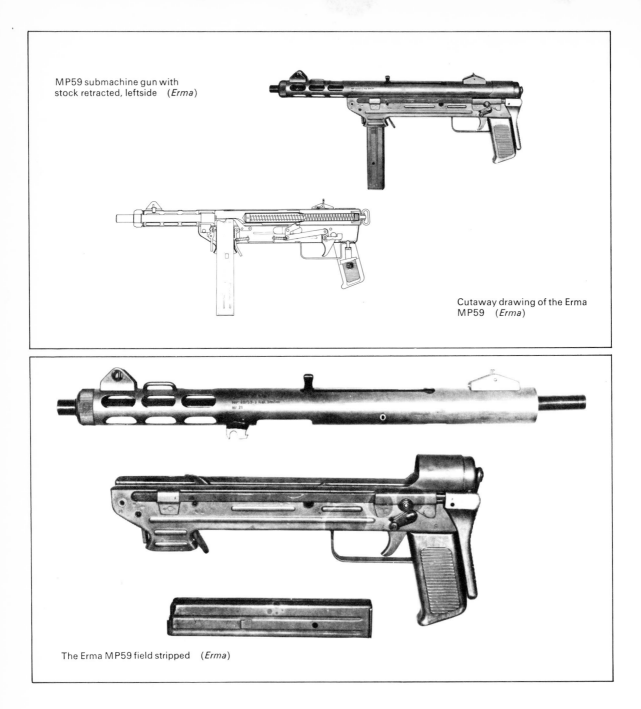

MP59 submachine gun with stock retracted, leftside (*Erma*)

Cutaway drawing of the Erma MP59 (*Erma*)

The Erma MP59 field stripped (*Erma*)

potential. The newly developed double line magazine used in the MP59 was discarded and the already fully-developed and extremely reliable Carl Gustav one substituted. The MP60 was presented for trial in June 1960. In private trials carried out by the firm the weapon had been found to be particularly reliable under sustained firing tests. Both the gun and the magazine, as was expected, proved trouble-free under sandy and muddy conditions. In fact Erma were confident enough to say that an optimum in efficiency had been reached. Ten MP60s were delivered in September 1960 to the Bundeswehr as troop test weapons, and during the course of the next two months, twenty more were hand-built. Erma felt that no changes were now

necessary as the optimum had been reached for a submachine gun in their experience, given the then existing military requirements. Once more the weapon had only a limited success.

MP65

Erma Werke felt that although it was *the* weapon for the late 1950s on all counts, it was possible with the experience gained and the changing military requirements that an improvement might be made and thus the MP65 was announced.
The improvements incorporated were a safety catch, operable from left or right, a shoulder stock which enabled the gun to be fired either left or right handed, single or full auto fire and optional sighting

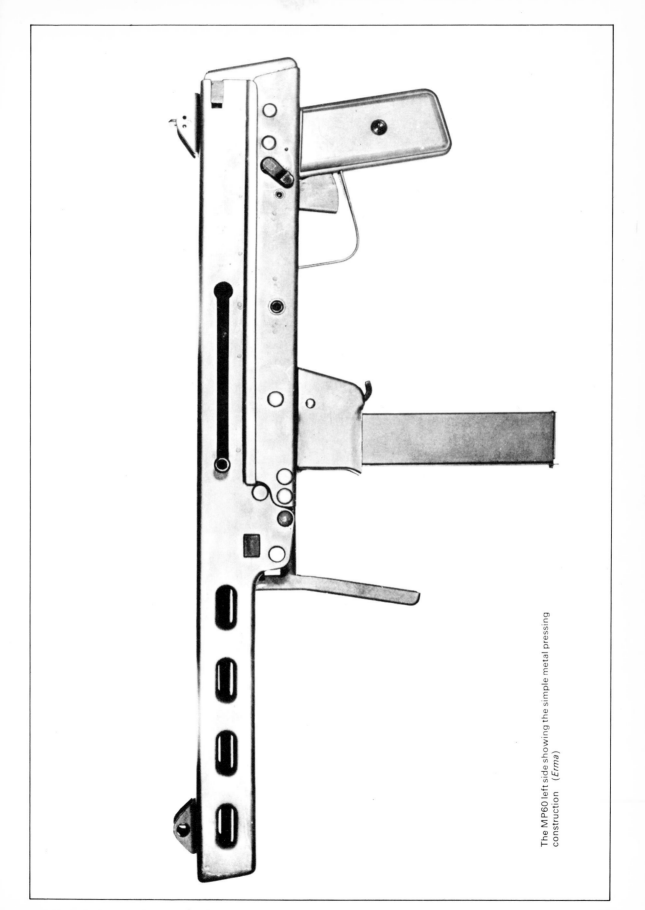

The MP60 left side showing the simple metal pressing construction   (*Erma*)

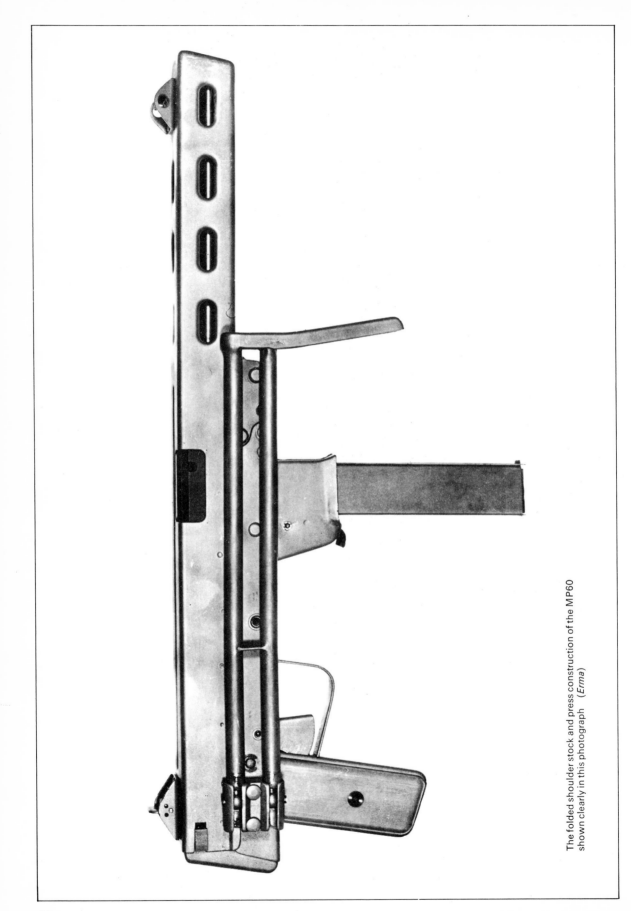

The folded shoulder stock and press construction of the MP60 shown clearly in this photograph   *(Erma)*

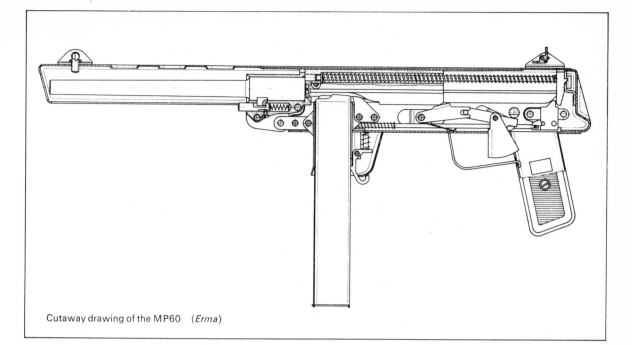

Cutaway drawing of the MP60   (*Erma*)

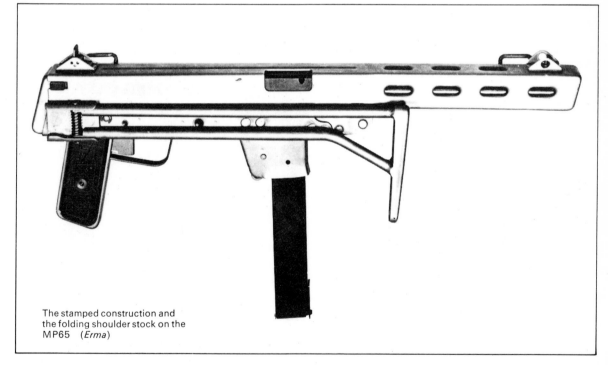

The stamped construction and
the folding shoulder stock on the
MP65   (*Erma*)

methods. The weapon had a number of safety
features which made it one of the safest submachine
guns produced. It can be easily stripped without
any tools, the barrel is easily and quickly changed
and the weapon is to all intents impervious to sand
and mud. It follows the now standard and well-tried
pattern of using simple and minimal machining
with many metal stampings welded together.
In conclusion it can only be said that Erma must be
admired for their perseverance in the face of
extreme difficulties, brought about by an army
whose requirements and test procedures varied
each time a new weapon was designed. The final
weapon produced is one that fulfils all the requirements for a submachine gun, being developed by a
firm with few, if any, rivals in experience of production and combat testing. This weapon although
deserving to be more successful than its pre-
decessors has met with the same lack of interest and
although minor modifications have been carried out
and many possible sales investigated the development has been suspended.
It would seem inconceivable that a firm such as
Erma will continue to produce no acceptable
military weapons and one can only wait expectantly
for their future developments.

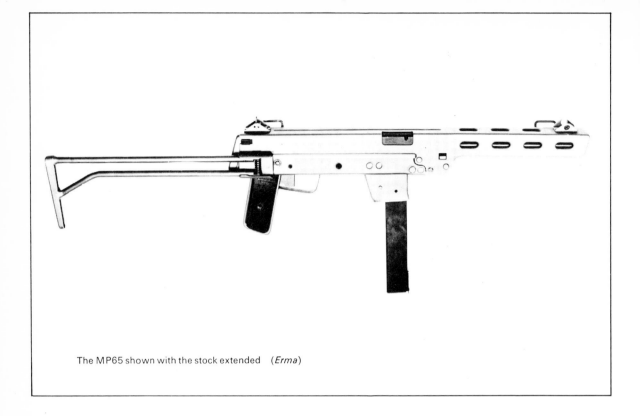

The MP65 shown with the stock extended   (*Erma*)

ERMA SUBMACHINE GUNS SPECIFICATIONS

Model	Calibre	Magazine Capacity	Weight	Rate of Fire rpm	Barrel Length	Length with Stock Folded	Extended
Vollmer	9mm Para 7·65mm Para 7·63mm Mauser	20/32/40/50	4·0kg	600	200mm/320mm	—	950mm
EMP	9mm Para	20/32	4·154kg	350-450	250mm	—	892mm
MP38/40	9mm Para	32	3·70kg	500-550	220mm	610mm	820mm
MP41	9mm Para	32	3·70kg	Unknown	251mm	—	864mm
MP44	9mm Para	64 (2×32)	3·632kg	Unknown	250mm	—	721mm
PM9	9mm Para	32	2·538kg	750	213·36mm	259mm	639mm
MP56	9mm Para	32	3·5kg Police 4·4kg Military	500-550	260mm	440mm	740mm
MP57	9mm Para	32	3·8kg	680-700	230mm	490mm	760mm
MP58	9mm Para	32	3kg	680-700	165mm	460mm	700mm
MP59	9mm Para	30	3·2kg	620-650	210mm	490mm	730mm
MP60	9mm Para	32	3·3kg	500-550	240mm	520mm	790mm
MP65	9mm Para	36	3·3kg	500-550	240mm	520mm	790mm

Acknowledgements
The author wishes to extend his thanks to Erma for
assistance in supplying material for this Profile.

An Irish soldier in the jungle of Burma equipped with a
Thompson submachine gun Model 1928   (*IWM*)

Thompson Submachine Gun

A. J. R. Cormack

"We're off to Dublin in the green,
in the green,
Where helmets glisten in the sun;
Where the bayonets flash, and the
rifles crash
To the echo of a Thompson gun."
Dominic Behan.

The Thompson submachine gun was named after
General John T. Thompson, a Director of Auto
Ordnance Corporation. Despite the fact that for at
least the first part of its history, the weapon was not
a commercial success its name became a household
word and it received a great deal of publicity. This
publicity, however, was not the kind that the pro-
ducers had in mind ! What self-respecting gangster
in a film would appear without his Tommy gun ?
Even the sale of the Thompson to the Law Enforcement Agencies did not make it respectable nor make
the fortune of Auto Ordnance. It was not until long
after the Prohibition era that the Thompson lost its
image as the gangland weapon and it was only the
advent of the Second World War that made the
Thompson a volume-produced weapon. Thompson
died in 1940 at the age of 80, and so lived to see this
success.

Auto Ordnance was formed by J. T. Thompson in
conjunction with Commander John Bliss and
Thomas Ryan in 1916 and had its offices in New
York City. The Thompson submachine gun was a
joint design, although credited by some to John
Thompson alone. Thompson did, however,
certainly originate the term submachine gun as well
as giving the Thompson its name. After the death of

The Thompson submachine gun in its well-known environment at the hands of an American policeman
(*Numrich Arms Corp NAC*)

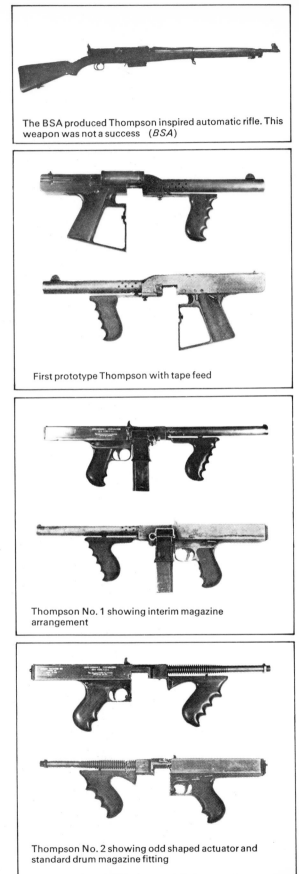

The BSA produced Thompson inspired automatic rifle. This weapon was not a success (*BSA*)

First prototype Thompson with tape feed

Thompson No. 1 showing interim magazine arrangement

Thompson No. 2 showing odd shaped actuator and standard drum magazine fitting

Thomas Ryan he left Auto Ordnance in 1928. The firm was then taken over by Russell Maguire of Maguire Industries and remained in their hands until December 1951 when George Numrich Junior acquired the name and spares for the Numrich Arms Corporation.

Prototypes

After an abortive attempt to develop a ·30 calibre automatic rifle it was decided to start a submachine gun design. The original Thompson prototype is an odd-looking weapon and, from what can be ascertained (the records are incomplete), was belt-fed with a butt and had two pistol grips. The gun had a very high rate of fire, over 1000rpm, and was chambered for ·45 ACP cartridges. The belt advancing mechanism was on the right side of the weapon. The prototype production, which started some time before 1919, was at the plant of Warner and Swassey. This early prototype would seem to have no relation to the later guns other than the 'H' piece in the lock. The 'H' piece in the above weapon was made of steel unlike that of the later weapons.

Model 1919

In 1919 the first proper Thompson, the Model 1919, was produced. This gun had a box magazine and pistol twin grips ; the lack of a stock would seem to rule out accurate shooting to say nothing of the lack of sights ; later weapons were made with sights and a stock. As there were only a very few, possibly only one, of each modification produced, all Model 1919 guns can be classed as prototypes. One technical feature, which appeared then, was a fixed firing pin. This was dropped and then reinstated in later models. The hesitation lock system, which depended on the adhesion of an angled surface to hold the 'H' piece into engagement with locking slots was a design feature which Captain John Bliss of the US Navy patented on 30 June 1913.

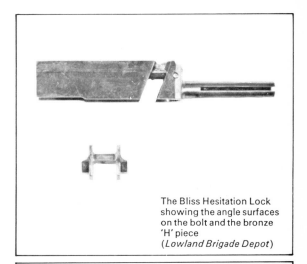

The Bliss Hesitation Lock showing the angle surfaces on the bolt and the bronze 'H' piece
(*Lowland Brigade Depot*)

Cased Thompson submachine gun Model 1921 manufactured by the Auto Ordnance Corp. Notice the case can accommodate 100-round drum when the adaptor is removed
(*Smithsonian Inst*)

Model 1921

In 1920 the Thompson was demonstrated to the military at Camp Perry. The results of this demonstration were to be far-reaching because, as a result of the enthusiasm shown by the military, Auto Ordnance contracted with Colt to produce the parts for 15,000 Model 21 submachine guns. This

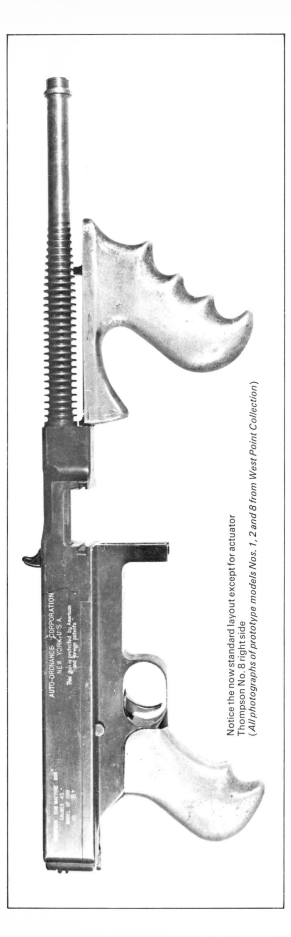

Notice the now standard layout except for actuator
Thompson No. 8 right side
(*All photographs of prototype models Nos. 1, 2 and 8 from West Point Collection*)

AUTO-ORDNANCE CORPORATION
NEW YORK·U·S·A·
This gun is protected by American and Foreign patents

Model 1921 Thompson submachine gun with Colt markings
fitted with a 20-round box magazine
(*Lowland Brigade Depot*)

Thompson Model 1921 with 20-round box magazine fitted and
a 50-round drum magazine below. Notice the raised Lyman
backsight
(*Lowland Brigade Depot*)

enthusiasm, however, was not maintained and, in fact, these 15,000 basic guns were to provide parts for a succession of later models. They lasted Auto Ordnance for nearly 20 years !

The Model 21 had a detachable butt, Lyman adjustable sights, and a box magazine. The 50- and 100-round drum magazines were still offered as an option to this 20-round box magazine. By modifications to the bolt the cyclic rate was reduced from 1000 rounds per minute to 800 rounds per minute,

as it had been found that on fully automatic fire the gun was not easily controlled. Sales were not impressive ; only sample lots to various Governments and a few to small law enforcement agencies kept the production line moving. The sales drive included offers of the weapon in a variety of calibres. The Model 1921 continued to be offered for sale by Auto Ordnance as late as 1933. The Thompson was not having a commercial success. The gun weighs 9·75lb, has an overall length of 31·8in and a 10·5in barrel.

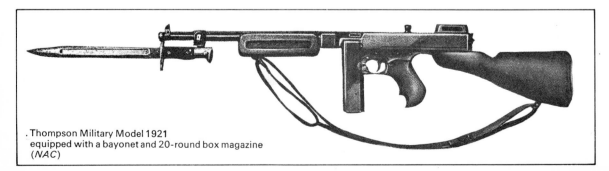

. Thompson Military Model 1921
equipped with a bayonet and 20-round box magazine
(*NAC*)

66

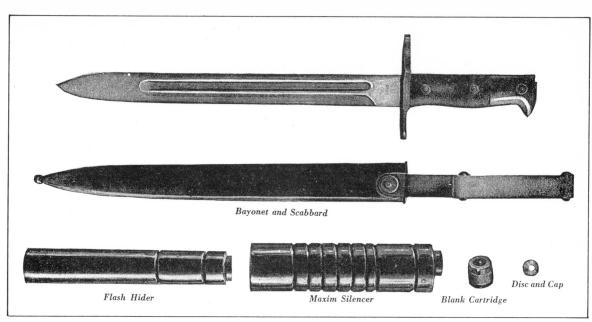

Bayonet and Scabbard

Flash Hider   Maxim Silencer   Blank Cartridge   Disc and Cap

The accessories available for Model 1921 including bayonet,
flash hider, silencer and a blank cartridge adaptor
(*NAC*)

Model 1923

In 1923 a rare and technically interesting variation
was introduced. The Model 23 was, as far as can be
ascertained, never marketed in quantity and as a
result the few which were manufactured are
collector's pieces. The cartridge, which was designed in conjunction with Remington and called
the Remington-Thompson ·45, was an attempt to
provide a submachine gun with more than the
power of a standard pistol round. This cartridge was
an elongated and uprated ·45 ACP, the case being
one inch long and the bullet weighing 250 grains.
This, coupled with a muzzle velocity of 1450fps,
makes it a truly powerful round, compared with the
·45 ACP with its 180 grain bullet and 850fps. A
special magazine was needed and the one used
with the shot cartridge, which took 18 of them, was
probably used.

The catalogue for the 1921-23 Thompson shows

that there were also offered as alternative cartridges :
·351 (a cartridge offered by Winchester for the 1907
Winchester self-loading rifle), 9mm Mauser (this
was a powerful, straight-sided case offered by
Mauser as an export option on the Broomhandle),
9mm parabellum (the most popular of all submachine gun rounds), and the Thompson shot
cartridge. It is doubtful whether these calibres were
ever made in quantity.

In 1952 Numrich Arms sold a number of Thompson
finned barrels in calibres 9mm Luger, 7·63 Mauser
and ·30 Luger. It is possible that these were originally intended for the Model 1923. Once again the
parts for this gun were modified from the 1921
Model with a new lengthened 20-shot box
magazine.

The Model 1923 was also offered as a military
model, with a 16in Springfield bayonet and bipod.
It is worth quoting some passages from the cata-

The cartridges which were offered for the Model 1923. It is
doubtful whether the weapon was in fact chambered for all
these cartridges   (*NAC*)

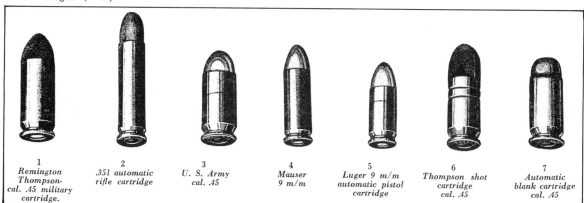

1	2	3	4	5	6	7
Remington Thompson-cal. .45 military cartridge.	*.351 automatic rifle cartridge*	*U. S. Army cal. .45*	*Mauser 9 m/m*	*Luger 9 m/m automatic pistol cartridge*	*Thompson shot cartridge cal. .45*	*Automatic blank cartridge cal. .45*

Thompson military model submachine gun 1923 with bipod
fitted. Notice the smooth barrel jacket and lack of forward
pistol grip
(*NAC*)

There were various mounts specified for use with the Thompson
submachine gun. Illustrated above is the motor-cycle sidecar
variation
(*NAC*)

logue. 'A rate of 125 accurately aimed shots per
minute can be easily attained !' and 'an unlimited
number of rounds can be fired without bruising or
shocking the body'. This fact was probably some
consolation to the man who fired '3000 rounds
without overheating'. It 'has a fire power equivalent
to a squad or more of men armed with hand loaded
military muskets !' A final and by no means
warranted boast : 'The Thompson Gun when thus
used is more accurate than a pistol, safer than a
rifle and more effective than a shotgun.' This was in
police work ! The model 1923 had an overall length
of 36in and had a 14·5in barrel.
One of the most bizarre projected uses of the
1921-23 was the forerunner of the 'gunships' of
the Vietnam war. This was the mounting of no less
than 28 Thompsons in the floor of an aircraft to give
strafing power. This layout fired at an estimated
45,000rpm covering an area of 5280sq.yds in six
seconds. The two further guns carried in the cockpits
would seem to have been superfluous. A few sales
of this type would have made the fortune of Auto
Ordnance !

Below and top left of facing page:
The forerunner of the Vietnam War Gunship. Thompson
submachine guns mounted in banks in an aircraft
(*NAC*)

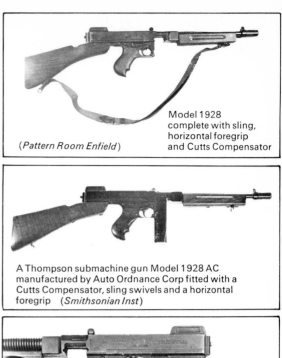

Model 1928 complete with sling, horizontal foregrip and Cutts Compensator
(*Pattern Room Enfield*)

Model 1927

The Model 1927 was another attempt to use up Model 1921 parts held in stock and was a semi-automatic version of the 1921. Why Auto Ordnance thought that a submachine gun that fired semi-automatic would sell better than a fully automatic one cannot be explained. The only possible explanation was that, as it was sold in very small numbers to Police Departments and private individuals, it was looked upon as a carbine rather than a submachine gun. The markings on the receiver rather bear this out as the 'Model 1927' and 'Thompson semi-automatic carbine' were stamped on it, and Model 1921 machined off. There were a large number of odd letter codes on the 1927 and these should not be mistaken for model numbers (Model 27 SCDS—S=Special Grade, C=Cutts Compensator, D=Drum Magazine and S=Sling Swivels). This weapon can be very easily converted to the fully automatic version by the substitution of a few standard 1921/1928 parts.

Model 1928

The Government of the United States, in the form of the US Navy Department, finally ordered a small number of Thompsons for the Marine Corps Expeditionary Force in Nicaragua. This was in 1928 and the first military use after the enthusiasm shown at the original Camp Perry demonstrations. The Model 1928 was the basic 1921, once more with modifications. On the above version, often called the Navy Version, the forward pistol grip was deleted, a straight wooden fore-end substituted,

A Thompson submachine gun Model 1928 AC manufactured by Auto Ordnance Corp fitted with a Cutts Compensator, sling swivels and a horizontal foregrip (*Smithsonian Inst*)

Model 1928 manufactured by the Auto Ordnance Corp showing the magazine release, selector switch and safety. Notice the patent dates on the 20-round box magazine

Model 1928 showing the right side with a 20-round box magazine fitted, the finned barrel and a sling swivel fitted to the vertical foregrip

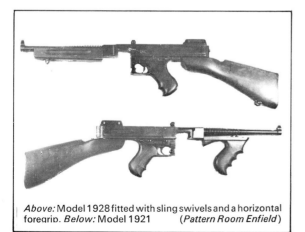

Above: Model 1928 fitted with sling swivels and a horizontal foregrip. *Below:* Model 1921 (*Pattern Room Enfield*)

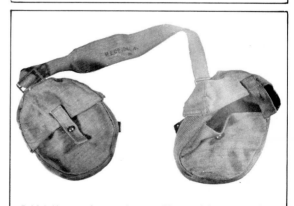

British Harness for carrying two 50-round drum magazines. notice the date 1941 (*Pattern Room Enfield*)

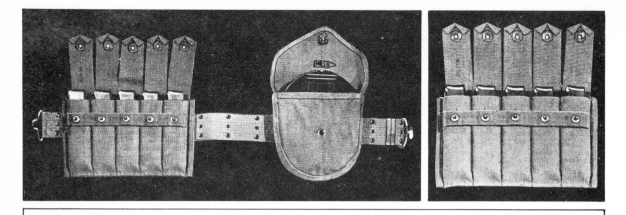

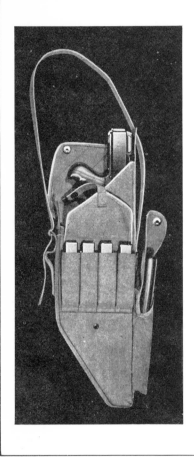

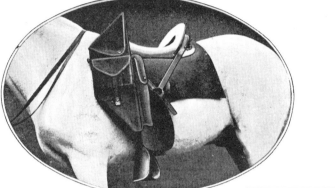

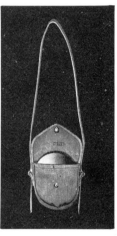

Various methods of carrying the Thompson submachine gun and its magazines were adopted. Illustrated are a number (*NAC*)

and sling swivels fitted. The rate of fire, which at 800rps was still found to be too fast, was slowed to 700rps by modifying the lock assembly once again and substituting a larger recoil spring. In an attempt to reduce the muzzle climb on fully automatic fire a Cutts Compensator was once again fitted. The Cutts Compensator worked on the principle of diverting the gases in an upward direction through slots at the end of the barrel and thus tending to force the muzzle downwards. It was designed by Colonel Richard M. Cutts and was introduced in 1926. All these weapons were restamped 'US Navy'.

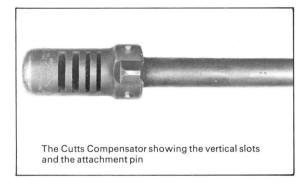

The Cutts Compensator showing the vertical slots and the attachment pin

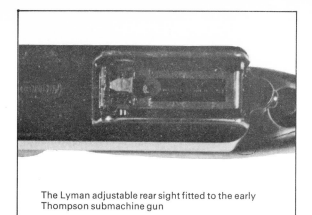

The Lyman adjustable rear sight fitted to the early Thompson submachine gun

Model 1928 A1

The US Cavalry, finding that it needed a weapon to equip its vehicle personnel, also adopted the Model 1928. The weapon was identical to the Navy Model 1928, but was stamped '1928 A1'. Even this contract cannot be called a great success, as only some 400 guns were ordered.

Auto Ordnance struggled on with a series of gadgets and modifications to make the Thompson a more attractive and marketable proposition. These gadgets included two interesting types of ammunition: the first a crowd control round which was a ·45 ACP case with an elongated capsule containing bird shot. The second, not so humane and

British soldier with full battle kit complete with a Thompson 1928 with vertical foregrip, Cutts Compensator and 50-round drum magazine
(*IWM*)

Above and below:
British soldiers equipped with Model 1928 Thompson submachine guns complete with sling, 20-round box magazine and Cutts Compensator
(*IWM*)

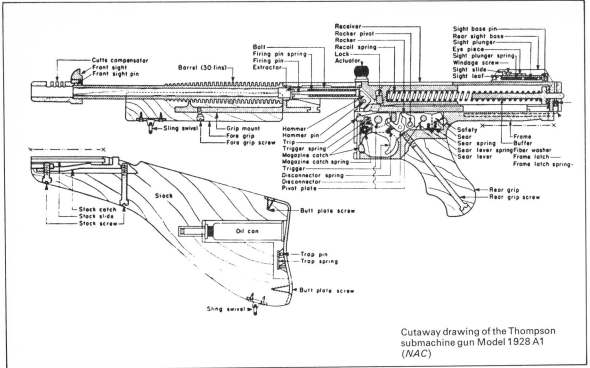

Cutaway drawing of the Thompson submachine gun Model 1928 A1 (*NAC*)

Royal Scottish Fusiliers posed for action in 1940. Notice the solider second from the left has the drum magazine winder missing (*IWM*)

A detachment of Coldstream Guards advancing equipped with full battle kit and Thompson submachine guns Model 1928. Notice the soldier in the foreground has the Lyman backsight raised (*IWM*)

presumably not intended for crowds, was a type of multiple ball round. It was made up of a core, a ball bearing and a jacket which, when fired split up and, in theory, tripled the effectiveness of the bullet. These were not new and were experimented with mostly with the same lack of success as they had had before. The 100-round drum magazine was dropped, as it was found that, apart from its feeding not being 100% reliable, it was too heavy and bulky.

The French Government were the first to order it for their Army, and in late 1939 they ordered 3750 Model 1928 weapons. But with the advent of World War Two and in particular, the retreat to Dunkirk, the British military changed their policy from one of not needing the gangsters' weapon to an urgent request for as many Thompson submachine guns as Auto Ordnance could supply. This request could not be met with any success by Auto Ordnance so they subcontracted to Savage Arms. This sub-contract continued until the American Government took over the responsibility for the supply of weapons to Britain in 1941 with the advent of Lease-Lend. Savage and Auto Ordnance continued to produce Thompson but under US Government contract.

Model 1928 A2

The 1928 A1 version of the Thompson was far from an ideal weapon for wartime production as it required extensive milling operations and hand finishing. Savage and Auto Ordnance made a detailed study as to how the weapon could be simplified. The result was the 1928 A2 model which had the pistol grips, the barrel cooling fins, the Cutts Compensator and the Lyman back sight, all deleted. Parts, e.g. the safety lever, were redesigned so that they could be produced on non-critical machines such as presses. All weapons produced at this time by Savage had serial numbers prefixed with an S, and those by Auto Ordnance with AO.

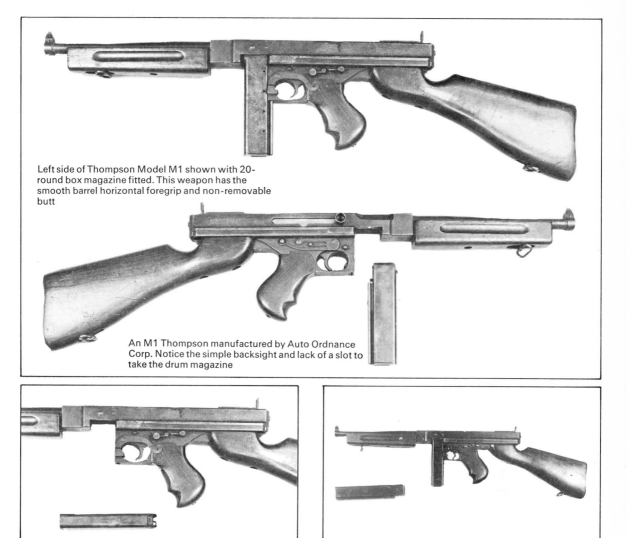

Left side of Thompson Model M1 shown with 20-round box magazine fitted. This weapon has the smooth barrel horizontal foregrip and non-removable butt

An M1 Thompson manufactured by Auto Ordnance Corp. Notice the simple backsight and lack of a slot to take the drum magazine

Thompson Model M1 showing the much simplified fire and safe levers. Notice also the magazine manufactured by the Crosby Co

Thompson Model M1 from an early production run showing the 1928 type of selector and safe lever also shown is the 30-round box magazine
(*Pattern Room Enfield*)

Thompson Model M1 early production weapon fitted with a silencer. Compare the size of the silencer used to give relatively good efficiency with that supplied originally
(*Pattern Room Enfield*)

Thompson Model M1A1 fitted with a sling. Notice the shielded rear sight
(*Pattern Room Enfield*)

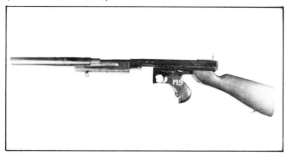

Model M1

The M1 Thompson saw the end of the Bliss delayed lock and the adoption of a simple blowback design. Contrary to the widely held opinion that the Thompson would function without the H piece, it not only will not, but the actuator does not move forward to chamber a round. *The ability to fire without the H piece is given as the reason for the development of the blowback version, but the deletion of the H piece and the oiler was a logical development when wartime conditions are borne in mind. Many parts remained interchangeable with

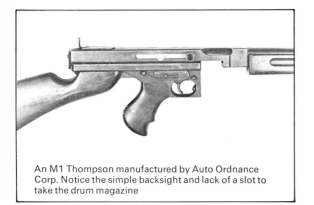

An M1 Thompson manufactured by Auto Ordnance Corp. Notice the simple backsight and lack of a slot to take the drum magazine

the earlier models but the drum magazine was abandoned and cannot be used on this weapon. One point to note is that the box magazines are loaded vertically into the gun but the box must be slid in from the side. One of the prime functions of the Bliss lock apart from any locking value was the fact that a considerable reduction in the rate of fire was achieved.

In 1942, an interim model, the 42M1, was produced in limited quantity. All weapons had, up till this time, been hammer-fired, i.e. there was a separate firing-pin which was struck by the hammer. On the 42M1 the hammer was deleted but a separate firing-pin integral with the bolt was retained.

---

*The Bolt Author's Note
The weapon cannot be cocked because the bolt will not move back unless by gravity. The Author has tried these manoeuvres out in the comfort of a barracks and cannot imagine them being practical under battle conditions.

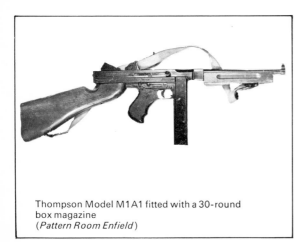

Thompson Model M1A1 fitted with a 30-round box magazine
(Pattern Room Enfield)

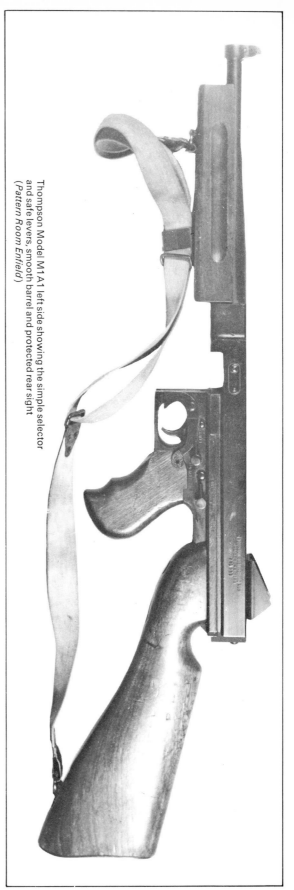

Thompson Model M1A1 left side showing the simple selector and safe levers, smooth barrel and protected rear sight
(Pattern Room Enfield)

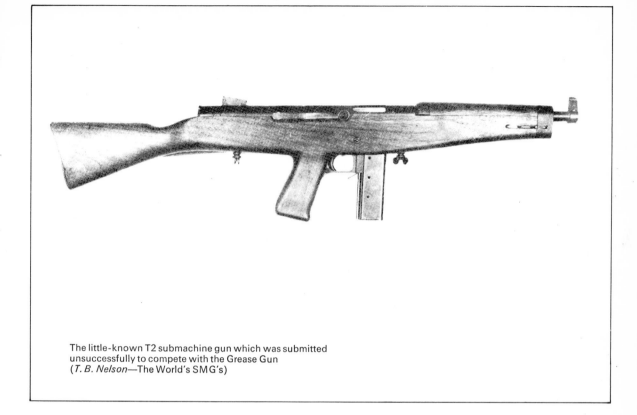

The little-known T2 submachine gun which was submitted
unsuccessfully to compete with the Grease Gun
(*T. B. Nelson*—The World's SMG's)

Model M1A1

The final version of the Thompson featured the
deletion of the separate pin and the substitution of
one machined on to the face of the bolt. There were
some 515,000 manufactured before the availability
of the M3A1 'Grease Gun' became sufficient for the
Thompson to be relegated to the status of a
'limited standard weapon'.

A number of experimental weapons were manufactured before and during the war. The Thompson was
chambered for the M1 carbine cartridge and also for
9mm parabellum. A ·22 conversion unit, designed
by Robbins was available, but only one or two are
known to have survived the war.

During 1942, when the search for a simple submachine gun was in full swing Auto Ordnance
submitted a gun designed by W. D. Hammond,
called the T2. This featured a simple tube receiver
minimum number of components and was a simple
blowback design. The 31 components cost only
50 dollars to make and the ·45 calibre gun used the
standard Thompson box magazines and the
alternative 9mm version a special one. The wood
fore-end almost covered the receiver and the
weapon weighed 8lb. The weapon was rejected
because it suffered a large number of breakages
during the tests.

The Thompson was copied by many nations, the
best known copy being the Chinese. Some of these
weapons were manufactured at the Chinese
Military Arsenal at Shansi during the mid 1930s.
All weapons are easily recognised by the profusion
of Chinese letters on the receivers.

Magazines

The basic magazines which were available were two
box and two drum with the addition of a box for the
riot cartridge. They were designated as follows:

20-round box type XX   50-round drum type L
30-round box type XXX   100-round drum type C
18-round box for riot cartridge XVIII

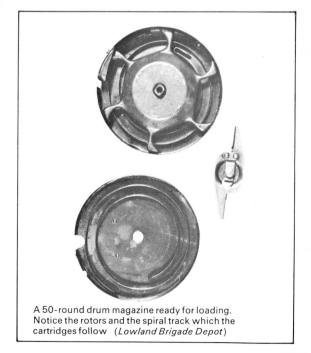

A 50-round drum magazine ready for loading.
Notice the rotors and the spiral track which the
cartridges follow (*Lowland Brigade Depot*)

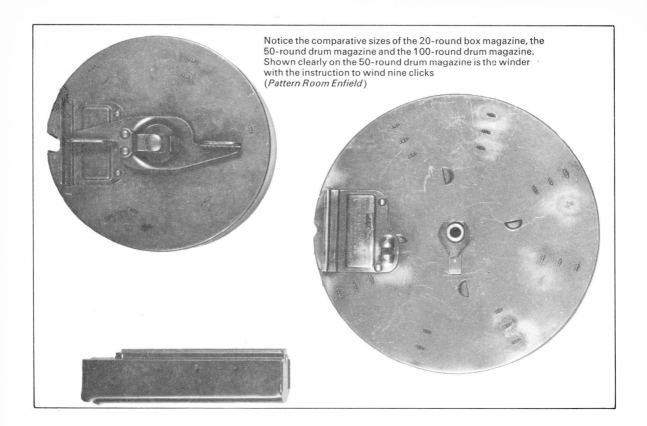

Notice the comparative sizes of the 20-round box magazine, the 50-round drum magazine and the 100-round drum magazine. Shown clearly on the 50-round drum magazine is the winder with the instruction to wind nine clicks
(*Pattern Room Enfield*)

The magazines weigh as follows:
Empty drum 50 round   2·63lb
Empty box 20 round   ·38lb
Full drum 50 round   4·95lb

Full box 20 round   1·31lb
The fact that the 100-round drum was abandoned for unreliable feeding would seem only one of the reasons when one considers the loaded weight.

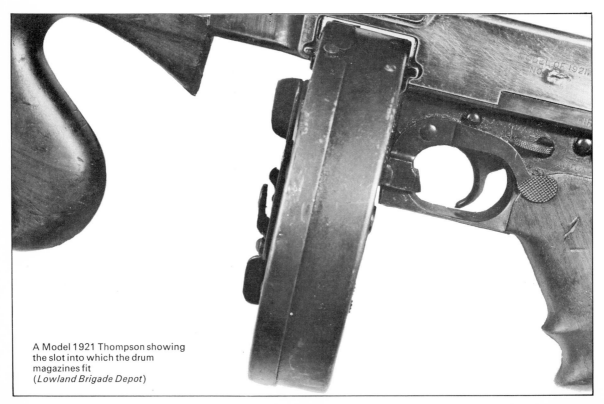

A Model 1921 Thompson showing the slot into which the drum magazines fit
(*Lowland Brigade Depot*)

A crude copy of an M1 Thompson manufactured by
the Viet-Cong. Notice how closely the basic outline
follows the M1
(*West Point*)

BSA-produced Thompsons

The Birmingham Small Arms Company modified the basic 1921 model in 1926 by fitting a selector switch for semi/fully automatic fire and chambering it for 9mm parabellum. The BSA 1926 model serial number 2 is 32in long and weighs 7½lb. It is in 9mm parabellum. The trigger guard was moved back and the butt attached to the back of the receiver, as opposed to the bottom on the Auto Ordnance produced weapons. Some of the features of the BSA would seem to have been used in the Auto Ordnance model 1928 indicating that there was some co-operation between the two firms.

In 1929 the Belgian Government ran a competition to find the most suitable submachine gun for their Army. BSA and Auto Ordnance decided to co-operate with an entry. This was the 1929 BSA model of which the following serial numbers are known:

No. 2—Calibre ·45 ACP 700rpm ; Weight 10½lb. Length 35·37in with a Cutts Compensator fitted.

No. 4—Similar to the No. 2 but chambered for the Belgian 9mm Bayard cartridge.

No. 7—7·63 Mauser : Weight 9¾lb with a forward curved magazine.

No. 8—The same as the above but stamped ·30 Mauser.

Post-1951 Numrich Arms have continued to sell the Thompson Model M1A1 to law enforcement

A variety of BSA produced Thompson submachine guns.
Notice the small variations in design between each model
(*T. B. Nelson*—The World's SMG's)

agencies and to foreign Governments. They also assembled a number of Model 1921/28 from spares. During 1954 Numrich made an experimental version for the M1 carbine cartridge but this was not put into production. Many rumours have been circulated about the legal semi-automatic version going into production again, but nothing has come of these yet. Many copies of the Thompson have been made ranging from 'official' Chinese copies to the two Vietnamese weapons illustrated. However the Thompson is still in active service with the South Vietnamese Army and it would seem that like any good soldier it will never die.

A relatively well manufactured copy of the Thompson submachine gun made in a jungle workshop by the Viet-Cong
(*West Point*)

A Viet-Cong copy of a Thompson submachine gun showing a variety of features from different models. The weapon was captured from the Viet-Cong
(*West Point*)

The successor to the Thompson submachine gun—The Grease Gun
(*Pattern Room Enfield*)

Close up of Model 1921 markings   (*Lowland Brigade Depot*)

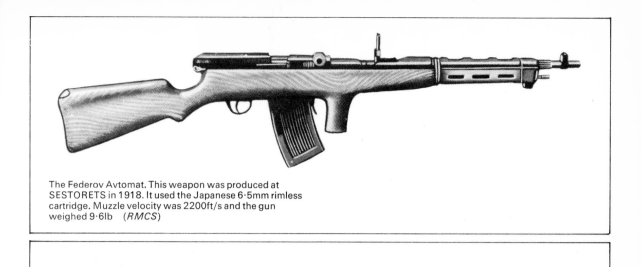

The Federov Avtomat. This weapon was produced at SESTORETS in 1918. It used the Japanese 6·5mm rimless cartridge. Muzzle velocity was 2200ft/s and the gun weighed 9·6lb   (*RMCS*)

The PPD 1940. Used in the Battles of the Lakes in the campaign against the Finns. It can be distinguished from the PPD 34/38 by a re-designed magazine housing and the new 71-round drum which has no extension piece.

Russian Submachine Guns

by Major F. W. A. Hobart (Retd)[1]

The Russians made greater use of the submachine gun than ony other army during World War II. In part this was forced upon them by the loss of a great deal of their manufacturing capacity as the Germans moved eastwards during the summer and autumn of 1941. Operation 'Barbarossa' was initially so successful that the machine tools were simply no longer available to the Russians to manufacture small arms in the quantities required. Simple designs utilizing pressings and stampings and not needing extensive machining operations were adopted from 1942 onwards. Once however these weapons were available the Russians made tremendous use of them and even went to the extreme length of equipping entire battalions of tank riders who were armed with no other weapon. The troops, as their name implies, gave the closest possible support to armoured units and provided the intimate co-operation between infantry and tanks

without which the latter cannot operate successfully —particularly in close country where enemy infantry are able to use short range anti-tank weapons with relative impunity. The SMG was also employed extensively in the infantry battalion where commanders and two or three others of the eight man section were equipped with this type of weapon. It was used by armoured units, gun detachments, drivers and supply troops.
The total number of SMGs made by the Soviet Union is not known but there is no doubt that it exceeded 10 million.

The Federov Avtomat
The first Russian weapon to resemble the modern accepted shape of the SMG was designed by Vladimir Grigorevitch Federov. He was born in St Petersburg in 1874 and always intended to adopt a military career. He entered the Artillery Academy in 1897 and graduated in 1900. In 1905 he produced a conversion of the Mosin-Nagant 7·62mm bolt-

[1] The views expressed are those of the author and do not reflect official opinion.

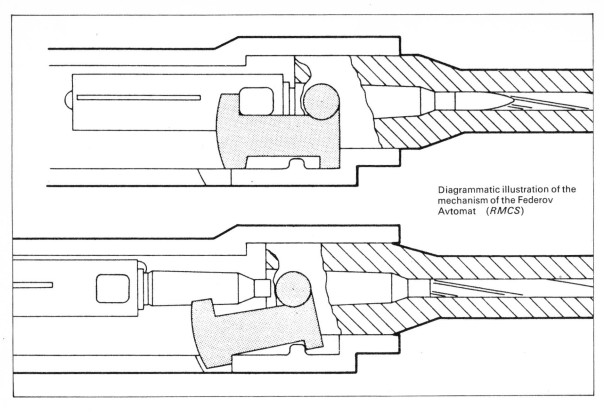

Diagrammatic illustration of the mechanism of the Federov Avtomat (*RMCS*)

action rifle to a self-loading action. This was never accepted in spite of trials carried out as late as 1926. During his work on the Mosin he concluded that using a cartridge of reduced impulse would permit the design of a lightweight rapid firing weapon. He chose to use the Japanese 6·5mm rimless round for three reasons. Firstly it produced the reduced impulse—compared with the 7·62mm×54R cartridge—secondly, its short case made automatic action and a short bodied weapon easier and, thirdly, the lack of a rim made magazine feeding much more reliable.

To enable the weapon to maintain accuracy when firing at its cyclic rate of 600 rounds/min he introduced a pistol grip forward of the magazine on which the firer could pull down to keep the muzzle from rising.

Federov used a system of short recoil operation for his weapon in which the barrel came back about ⅜in locked to the breech. Attached to the side of the barrel was a lever which struck a projection in the body and was pivotted to throw the breech block rearwards with increased velocity after unlocking occurred. The locking system consisted of a dumb-bell shaped piece mounted on the outer surface of each side of the chamber. The upper projections of the dumb-bell were the pivot at the front and the locking surface at the rear. The lower humps provided the pivoting surface at the front and the barrel latch at the rear. When the gun was ready to fire the upper projection was located behind

Vladimir Grigorevitch Federov,—Captain of Guards—Designer —Later chief of the Soviet Small Arms Design Office established at the Kovrov Machine Gun Factory in 1924 (*Novosti*)

a lateral projection from the side of the bolt which formed a locking stud. Thus when the bolt was blown backwards the barrel came back with it. After ⅜in of free travel to allow the pressure to drop to a safe low level, the lower front projection came into contact with a raised boss on the floor of the body and this rotated the locking piece down at its rear end and the bottom of the pivotting member entered a cut-away in the bottom of the body and stayed there. Thus whilst the accelerator increased the bolt velocity, the barrel remained latched to the rear. This is shown on the accompanying diagram. When the bolt came forward under the drive of the return spring it picked up the top round from the 25 round box-magazine and chambered it. The contact with the accelerator freed the locking-piece from the bottom of the body and as the barrel ran out the lock was carried up behind the bolt-locking stud and the gun was ready to fire again.

The muzzle velocity of this weapon was 2200ft/s and with a weight of 9·6lb it could well be claimed— as some authorities do—that this is the first assault rifle and not a true SMG. However there is no doubt that in the fighting that went on in 1919 between the White Russians, assisted by their Western Allies, and the Red Armies, the 3000 Avtomats produced at Sestorets were used in a role which was that of a SMG.

All subsequent Soviet submachine guns were blowback operated. In this method the barrel is fixed securely to the body of the gun and cannot therefore move relative to it. The gun fires from an unlocked breech and so the cost and complication of making a breech locking system is avoided. Throughout the period 1934-1945 all Soviet SMGs used the 7·62mm cartridge which had a case length of 25mm. This is generally known as the 'P' cartridge and it is basically a pistol cartridge with all the limitations that implies. (See Ammunition Profile No 12). The case is semi-bottle-necked and has a long near parallel sided case from the neck to the extractor groove which provides obturation during the blowback operation.

In blowback operation the bolt is held to the rear when the gun is in the 'ready' position and the ammunition is held in the magazine. When the trigger is operated the bolt goes forward, collects a round from the magazine and forces it into the chamber. The actual mode of firing can be by one of two methods. Either the bolt face carries a fixed firing pin or—less often—the firing pin is driven forward when the bolt is in the closed position, by some external control mechanism. The fixed firing pin has the advantage of cheapness in manufacture and simplicity in operation. The controlled firing pin although a more expensive feature does ensure that regularity of position of primer ignition is obtained.

The 1926 Tokarev SMG. This appeared in prototype only. The 7·62mm Nagent rimmed revolver cartridge was not a success   (RMCS)

This SMG is described by official Russian sources as the Tokarev SMG model 1931. Apart from this description nothing is known of it. The similarity with the Degtyarev 1940 is so great that there must be doubt as to the correctness of the Russian description (Novosti)

With the fixed firing pin the cartridge is not parallel to the bolt axis until it is partly chambered and so until this happens the cap and fixed firing pin cannot come into contact. When the round is lined up, firing will occur as soon as the frictional force between case and chamber wall holds up the case movement and the increased force on the cap from the pin fires it. This means that manufacturing tolerances on case and chamber can decide the moment of firing. A case on the largest permissible diameter and a chamber on the smallest dimensions will fire earlier than a small case in a large chamber. Dirt, sand or fouling will reduce the chamber diameter, increase the coefficient of friction and so cause early firing. In practice the cap is fired whilst it and the bolt are still moving forward.

Without going into too much detail this means that half the firing impulse is used to arrest the bolt and the other half to blow it back. This leads to a reduced bolt weight, a reduced rearward velocity and an acceptable rate of fire. It also leads to a slight variation in the moment of firing and therefore a difference in chamber volume and velocity but in the tactical role of the submachine gun this is of little importance.

The advantages of the blowback system can be seen to be simplicity of design, manufacture and construction allied with cheapness, effectiveness and simplicity of operation. These make it the ideal system for use with armies using large numbers of comparatively uneducated troops supplied by factories using simple cheap machinery operated by semi-skilled workers.

In 1926 a SMG was designed by Fedor Vasilevitch Tokarev. Tokarev was born in 1871 at Egorlikskaya. His parents were Cossacks and he became an apprentice to his village blacksmith when he was 11. When he was 14 he worked for a gun maker and in 1888 he became a trade student at the Novocherkassk Military Trade School, emerging after four years as a N.C.O. craftsman. He was posted to the 12th Don Cossack regiment. Four years later he returned to the Trade School as an Instructor in gun making. In 1907 he studied at the Officers' School at Oranienbaum. After graduation he served at the Sestorets Factory and in 1921 he went to the Tula Arsenal. His fame lies principally with his modification to the Maxim gun, his SL rifle of 1939, and his pistol which was in service until comparatively recently.

The Tokarev SMG fired the 7·62mm Nagent revolver cartridge at a rate of 1100-1200 rounds/minute. The rimmed round was not satisfactory and only experimental models were made. The arm can be recognised by its two triggers—one for single shot, one for full auto and the unusual shape of the magazine housing. A sketch of this weapon is shown.

The PPD 1934/38

The next SMG was the Degtyarev model of 1934. This was the PPD-1934/38. The designation PP—Pistolet Pulemet—meaning 'machine pistol' appears on all subsequent Soviet SMGs. All use the Russian 7·62mm × 25mm type P pistol cartridge. Vasily Degtyarev was born in Tula in 1890. He

Vasily Degtyarev. Major-General of Engineers, Doctor of Technical Sciences, Winner of four State Prizes, Deputy of the USSR Supreme Soviet. His Light Machine Gun armed Infantry, Tanks and Airmen. His SMGs were produced in large number (*Novosti*)

left school at 11 and was employed in Tula Arsenal operating a machine testing springs for the new Mosin rifle. He was drafted into the army and served at Sestorets Small Arms Factory where he worked under Federov. He later went to Oranienbaum where weapon testing was carried out. In 1916 he designed an automatic carbine. Little is known of this weapon except that it was not accepted during the Czarist regime. His chief claim to fame was the Degtyarev light machine gun which was produced in several versions and prodigious numbers for the Russian armies during World War II. He produced an anti-tank rifle and after the war came his RP46 and the RPD LMGs. He became a Major General of Engineers, Doctor of Technical Sciences, won four State Prizes, was a Deputy of the USSR Supreme Soviet and died in 1959 at the age of 69.

The PPD 1934/38 was a weapon based partly on an early Suomi design and partly on the Schmeisser MP-28. The magazine generally found on the gun is a 71-round drum magazine clearly copied from the Suomi. It is readily identified by the extension projecting above the drum, which fits into the receiver. It is said that some of the earlier magazines were of 73-round capacity and had a smaller number of feed followers. There is also a curved box

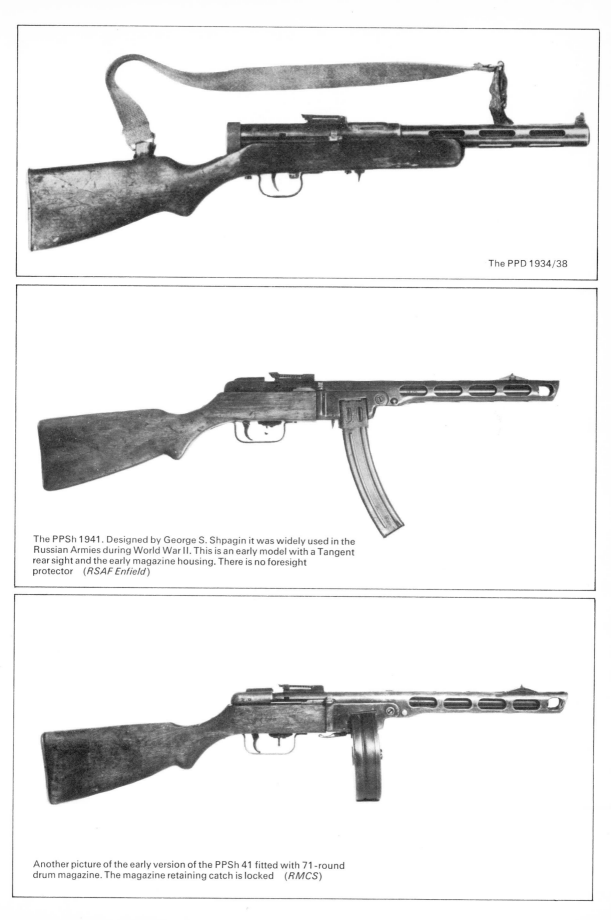

The PPD 1934/38

The PPSh 1941. Designed by George S. Shpagin it was widely used in the Russian Armies during World War II. This is an early model with a Tangent rear sight and the early magazine housing. There is no foresight protector   (*RSAF Enfield*)

Another picture of the early version of the PPSh 41 fitted with 71-round drum magazine. The magazine retaining catch is locked   (*RMCS*)

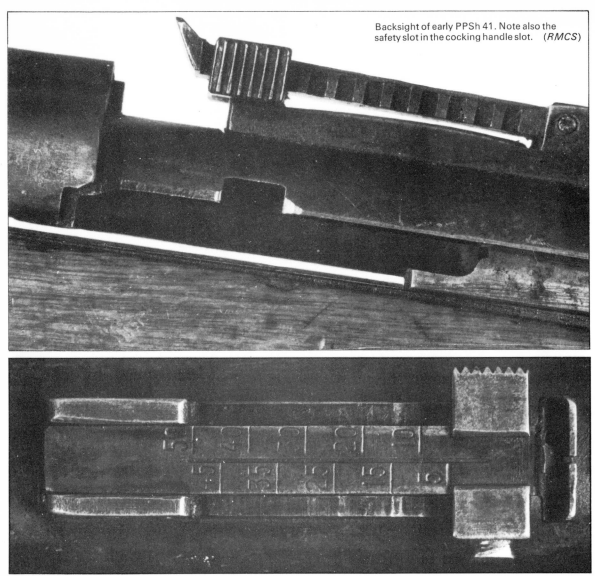

Backsight of early PPSh 41. Note also the safety slot in the cocking handle slot.   (*RMCS*)

Backsight of early PPSh 41. It was realised later that this close range graduation was totally unnecessary and a simple flip sight was introduced into later models   (*RMCS*)

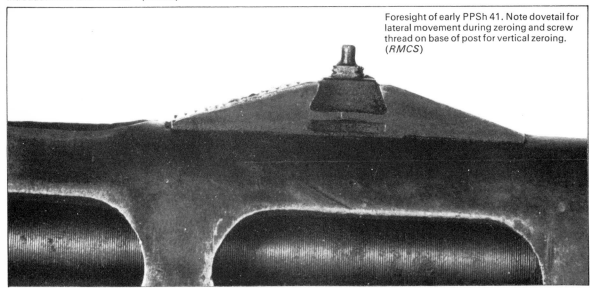

Foresight of early PPSh 41. Note dovetail for lateral movement during zeroing and screw thread on base of post for vertical zeroing. (*RMCS*)

magazine which held 25 rounds but this is rarely seen. The gun fires from an open breech and is of typical blowback design. One feature of interest is that both barrel and chamber are chrome-plated. The barrel jacket was machined from the solid and, in fact, there were neither pressings nor stampings employed in the construction of the gun.

There were several variations of the PPD 34/38 and it seems that they fitted into three main categories:

1 The earliest version took the 73-round magazine and the change lever, fitted in front of the trigger, was a 'flag' which could be rotated to show either '1' or '73'. The firing pin had an external cocking arrangement similar to the Schmeisser, the bolt was polished and the safety finger plate on the cocking handle was rounded. The trigger guard was of one piece construction. The ejection slot in front of the back sight was very narrow.

2 The standard gun took a 71-round drum and the change lever was so marked. There was a fixed firing pin and the bolt was blued. The safety plate was rectangular and the trigger guard was in two parts rivetted together. The ejection slot was much wider.

3 The late model differs from both the other models in having a barrel jacket with only three sets of slots as opposed to eight. Otherwise it is similar to the standard gun.

The PPD 34/38 was easy to fire and simply stripped. The milled cap at the rear of the receiver was unscrewed and the return spring and bolt were withdrawn.

The PPD 1940

The PPD—like its predecessor—was designed by Degtyarev and produced at Tula and Sestorets. It was used in the Finnish campaign and replaced the 34/38. The barrel housing is similar to that of the 34/38 but they are not interchangeable. It can be distinguished from the earlier gun by the wooden fore end in front of the magazine. The early model 1940 had a tangent rear sight like the 1934/38 but later versions had a simple V notch rear sight. The drum magazine does not have a vertical extension to fit into the gun but has a single lip fitting directly into the magazine holder in the receiver. There is also only one follower.

Although the receiver and cap, return spring, trigger mechanism and sling fittings are interchangeable with those of the 34/38, the bolt is not. This has a movable firing pin controlled by a lever on the bolt head which ensures that the bolt is fully closed before the round is fired.

The PPSh-41

The next submachine gun was designed by George S. Shpagin, Hero of Socialist Labour, and later Lieutenant-General in the Red Army. He collaborated with Degtyarev in producing a 12·7mm heavy machine gun which was used throughout World War II.

The PPSh-41 did not come into service until mid-1942 but the gun used stampings for the

George S. Shpagin, Hero of Socialist Labour and Lieut-General of the Red Army. He is best known for his work on the SMG and for his design of the feed mechanism for Degtyarev's 12·7mm machine gun (*Novosti*)

receiver and barrel jacket, the bolt was simple to construct and by the end of the war over five million guns had been made. It is now obsolete in the Soviet Army but has been manufactured in Hungary as the 48M, in North Korea as the Type 49 SMG and in China as the Type 50 SMG. The origin and date of manufacture of the weapon can be determined by the markings on top of the receiver. The back sight also helps in identification. Soviet and Iranian PPSh-41s have V back sights, North Korean Type 49 and Chinese Type 50 have aperture rear sights. All these weapons are basically the same except the North Vietnamese K50 which will be covered later. Some PPSh-41s were converted to 9mm during the war and some by Iran after the war. These are rare. The PPSh-41 is a blowback operated selective fire weapon with a wooden butt. The barrel is chromium plated and the weapon is extremely reliable and sturdy. The earliest Russian models had a tangent leaf rear sight but in late 1942 a simple flip over back sight, giving 100 or 200 metres, was introduced.

The magazine is either the 71-round drum of the PPD 40 or a 35-round slightly curved box magazine. The PPSh-41 is identified readily by the shape of the front end of the barrel jacket which extends beyond

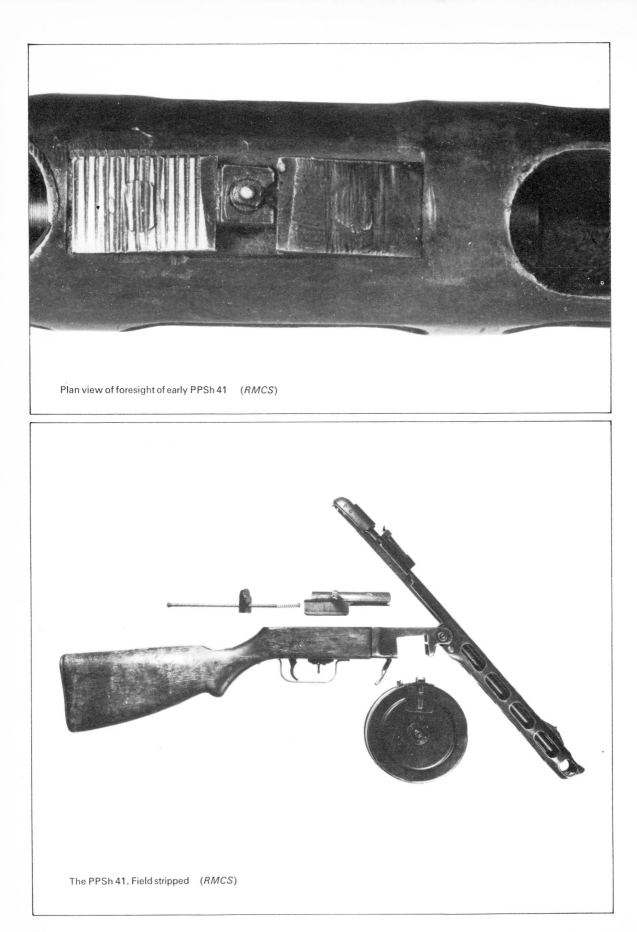

Plan view of foresight of early PPSh 41   (*RMCS*)

The PPSh 41. Field stripped   (*RMCS*)

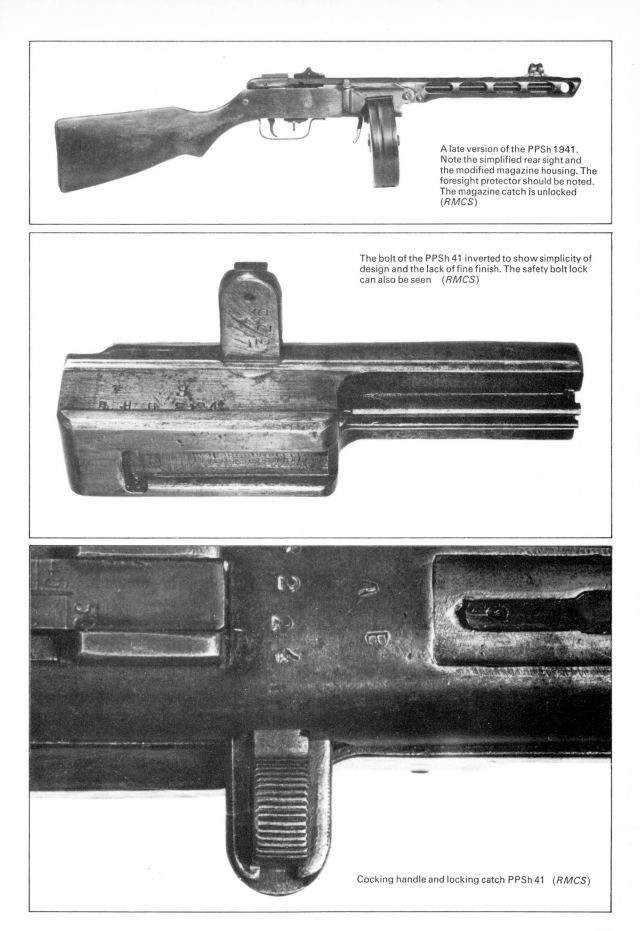

A late version of the PPSh 1941.
Note the simplified rear sight and
the modified magazine housing. The
foresight protector should be noted.
The magazine catch is unlocked
(*RMCS*)

The bolt of the PPSh 41 inverted to show simplicity of
design and the lack of fine finish. The safety bolt lock
can also be seen   (*RMCS*)

Cocking handle and locking catch PPSh 41   (*RMCS*)

Date marking on the top of the body of the PPSh 41. Note also the narrowness of the ejection opening. The coarse cut on the inside of the body is noticeable   (*RMCS*)

Trigger and safety catch PPSh 41
(*RMCS*)

Hungarian 48m—a direct copy of the later model of the PPSh 41 (*RSAF Enfield*)

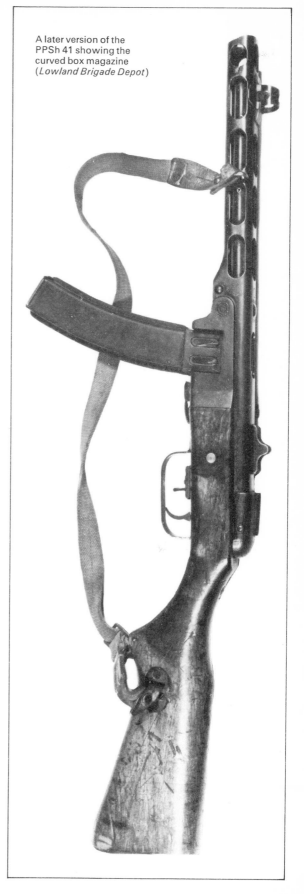

A later version of the PPSh 41 showing the curved box magazine (*Lowland Brigade Depot*)

the muzzle and is sloped back from top to bottom.
There is a gas exit port on the top so the extension
acts as a compensator to reduce muzzle climb at
full auto. The change lever is no longer a 'flag' but a
sliding catch enclosed within the trigger guard.
Pressing forward gives full automatic fire ; the
rearward position operates the disconnector to give
single shots. The cocking handle can be locked
either forward or to the rear.

The weapon can be stripped easily. After ensuring
safety, press forward on the receiver catch at the rear
of the body and swing the barrel down. Pull the
cocking handle rearward, rotate the bolt return
spring and buffer up and out of the receiver.

The drum magazines on the PPD and PPSh series
are not interchangeable on the gun but the procedure
for filling them is the same and is now described
in outline. Press the control button in the rear of the
drum and swing down the latch on the front cover of
the drum, lift off the cover and latch. Grasp the
cruciform rotor in the centre of the drum and wind the
spring two complete turns anti-clockwise. During
the first four clicks, which correspond to one
revolution, the cartridge conveyor must be held
stationary. The spiral track insert should now be
rotated as far as possible in an anti-clockwise
direction. Seventy-one rounds can now be placed
in the grooves of the spiral, bullet nose upwards.
When all the cartridges have been loaded grasp the
rotor and turn it slightly anti-clockwise against its
own spring ; at the same time press in the central
button to release the spring easing the rotor
clockwise until it stops. Replace the cover on the
magazine and place the latch back in the locked
position. It should be noted that the serial numbers
on the magazine and on the gun should coincide. If
they do not then it is best, if possible, to fire a few

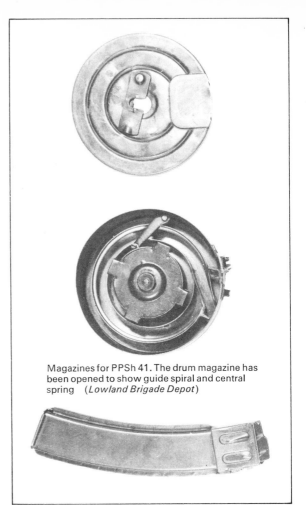

Magazines for PPSh 41. The drum magazine has
been opened to show guide spiral and central
spring   (*Lowland Brigade Depot*)

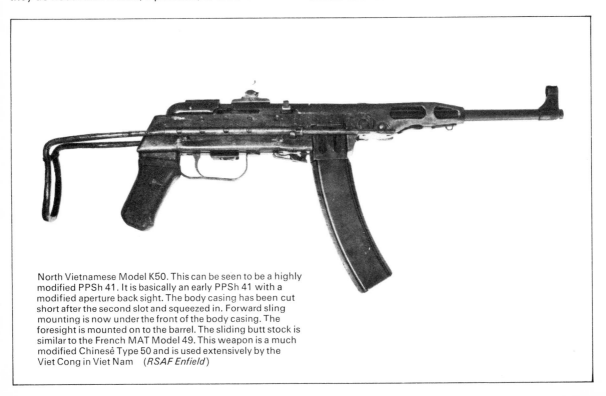

North Vietnamese Model K50. This can be seen to be a highly
modified PPSh 41. It is basically an early PPSh 41 with a
modified aperture back sight. The body casing has been cut
short after the second slot and squeezed in. Forward sling
mounting is now under the front of the body casing. The
foresight is mounted on to the barrel. The sliding butt stock is
similar to the French MAT Model 49. This weapon is a much
modified Chinese Type 50 and is used extensively by the
Viet Cong in Viet Nam   (*RSAF Enfield*)

The PPS-43. This is easily distinguished from the PPSh 41. The folding butt stock, uniquely shaped combination muzzle brake and compensator and position of safety catch provide ready recognition points   (*RCMS*)

The butt folded over the body. In this picture the shoulder piece has been folded forward about its pivot and as shown would foul the ejection slot. When the shoulder piece is correctly folded it lies over the backsight and behind the ejection slot   (*Lowland Brigade Depot*)

rounds to ensure functioning.

The SMG is loaded by inserting the drum or box magazine into the magazine opening and sliding it up into place until the magazine catch engages. The safety catch on the cocking handle is slipped out and after the cocking handle has been drawn to the rear the gun is ready to fire. The selector lever goes forward for automatic fire and rearward for semi-automatic. The cocked bolt can be held to the rear—if so required—by pushing in the safety catch on the cocking lever.

The sights can be set by flipping the leaf to '10' or '20' which represents 1 or 2 hundred metres. The bolt remains in the forward position when the ammunition is exhausted.

The K-50M SMG used by the Viet Cong is a modified Chinese Type 50 SMG which itself is derived directly from the PPSh-41. Firstly it fires either the Russian 7·62mm × 25mm Type P pistol cartridge or the 7·62mm × 25mm Type 50 Chinese pistol cartridge. The barrel jacket has been shortened and the muzzle compensator and fore grip have been eliminated. The lower part of the receiver has been changed in shape and a French pattern sliding

metal butt stock has replaced the original wooden stock.

The PPS-42

The PPS-42 was designed by A. I. Sudarev. Alexei Sudarev was born in August 1912 at Alatyr in central Russia. His father who was a telegraphist in the Kazan postal services died in 1924. Alexei was educated in a vocational-technical school and then worked in a factory as a fitter. He studied at a secondary school at Gorky. In 1932 he worked as a technician in the Urals and took out several Russian patents for engineering dumpers and tippers. In 1936 he became a student at Gorky Industrial Institute and in 1938 he was enrolled as a third year student at the Artillery Academy. In April 1940 Sudarev received a state scholarship and the rank of Lieutenant. Whilst at the Academy he designed an automatic pistol. In 1941 he became 'military engineer' 3rd class.

He was in Leningrad when the Germans beseiged it and designed, tested and carried out troop trials of a SMG known subsequently as the PPS-42.

The butt is released by pressing down on the pin above the rear of the body and can then be rotated upwards and over the body   (*RMCS*)

The PPS-43 field stripped   (*RMCS*)

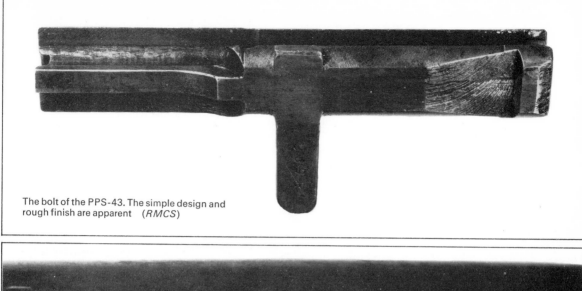

The bolt of the PPS-43. The simple design and rough finish are apparent   (*RMCS*)

Date of manufacture—May 1943 in this case—is shown on the body in front of the rear two-position U back sight. Note the greatly increased size of the ejection opening compared to that of the PPSh 41   (*RMCS*)

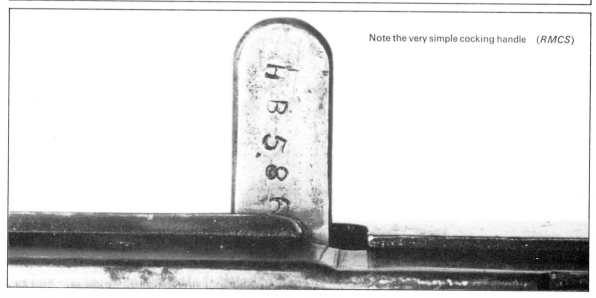

Note the very simple cocking handle   (*RMCS*)

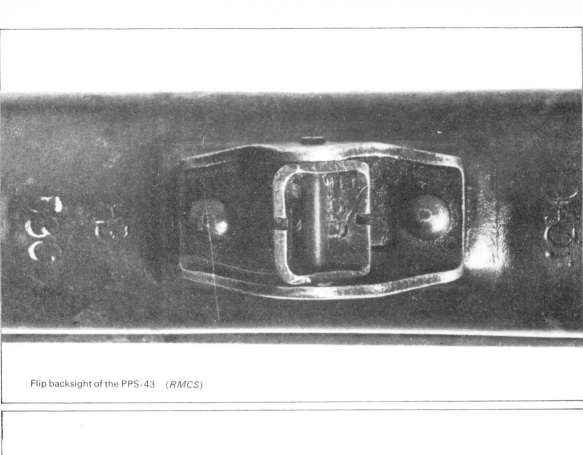

Flip backsight of the PPS-43   *(RMCS)*

Underneath view of muzzle brake on PPS-43   *(RMCS)*

Sudarev became ill in 1943 and died on 18 August 1946 at the age of 35. He had been awarded the Order of Lenin, the Order of the Patriotic War (1st class), the Red Star, and a State Prize. The gun is made of sheet steel of heavy gauge stamped into shape, rivetted and spot welded. The butt stock is of folding, metal design (except the Polish copy, the 43/52) and when it is folded this provides the easiest means of distinguishing it from the PPS-43. In the 42 the shoulder piece folds over and around the ejection port on top of the receiver. The stock of the PPS-43 has been shortened and lies behind the slot, when folded.

The gun was designed for quick production and simplicity. It uses only a simple 35 round box magazine which will NOT fit earlier guns. It fires only at full automatic but as the cyclic rate is reduced to 650rpm—from the PPSh-41 rate of 900—a skilled firer can manage single shots by dexterous trigger operation.
A sheet metal muzzle brake cum compensator of distinctive shape is attached to the front of the barrel jacket. The rear of it supports the muzzle. It is welded—NOT integral with the jacket as the PPSh-41—at the bottom of the jacket and rivetted at the top.

Foresight of PPS-43   *(RMCS)*

Alexei Sudarev designer of the PPS-43. He became ill in 1943 but continued to work from his bed until he died in 1946 aged 35   *(Novosti)*

The PPS-43

This is a Sudarev improved version of the PPS-42. It can easily be distinguished from the 42 by retracting the bolt. The return spring guide rod will be seen to project along the side of the bolt face to act as an ejector. Other differences from the PPS-42 are :

1 Safety is located forward of the trigger guard.

2 Magazine slopes forward at a steeper angle.

3 Folding stock is shorter.

4 Pistol grips are of rubber rather than wood. (Although some early models had wooden grips).

5 Muzzle brake is not welded to the bottom of the jacket but to an extra strap which gives support to the muzzle.

Stripping the 42 and 43 is straightforward. The receiver lock is above and behind the pistol grip which can be swung down when the lock is operated. Pull the cocking handle slightly back and then swing the bolt downward out of the receiver. Pull the return spring out of the bolt.

The PPS-43 is now obsolete in USSR but is still used in Poland as the Model 43/52 which differs in having a lengthened receiver and a rigid wooden butt. In China the PPS-43 is known as the Type 43 Copy—NOT as sometimes believed the Type 54 SMG.

The Soviet SMGs have been sturdy, well made, cheap, reliable and above all unsophisticated. They served the Union well and although they are no longer in service with the Red Army they are still in use with many Asian countries and have produced the greater part of the guerrilla armament in that continent.

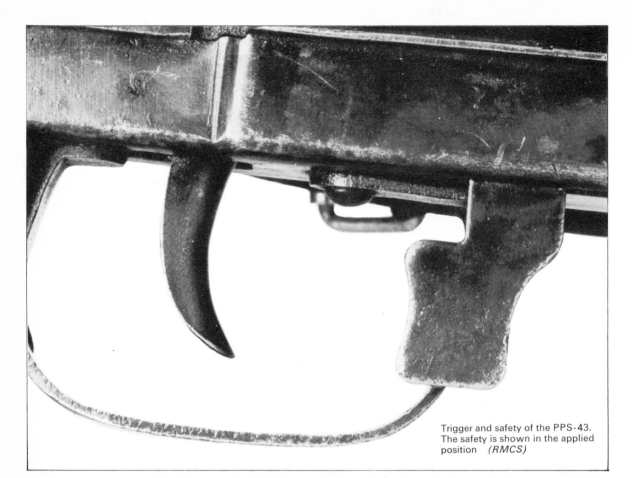

Trigger and safety of the PPS-43.
The safety is shown in the applied
position *(RMCS)*

TABLE OF RUSSIAN SMGs

	PPD 34/38	PPD 1940	PPSh 1941	PPS 42	PPS 43	K-50 Model[6]
Weights						
Weight (unloaded) (lb)	8·25	8·0	8·0	6·5	7·4	7·5
Weight of Loaded Magazine (lb)	4·25[1]	4·0[1]	4·0[1]	1·5	1·25	1·5
	1·0[2]		1·5[2]			
Weight Loaded (lb)	12·56[1]	12·0	12·0[1]	8·0	8·65	9·0
	9·25[2]		9·5[2]			
Lengths						
Overall (ins)	30·6	31	31·1	35·7[3]	32·25[3]	29·75[3]
				25·25[4]	24·25[4]	25·5[4]
Barrel (ins)	10·75	10·5	10·6	10·75	10·0	10·6
Mechanical Features						
Rifling Twist	RH	RH	RH	RH	RH	RH
No of Grooves	4	4	4	4	4	4
Method of Operation	Blow Back	Blow Back	Blow Back	Blow Back	Blow Back	Blow Back
Method of Feed	Magazine	Drum Magazine	Magazine	Box Magazine	Box Magazine	Box Magazine
Magazine capacity	Box 25	71	Box 35	35	35	35
	Drum 71		Drum 71			
Firing Characteristics						
Muzzle velocity (ft/s)	1600	1600	1600	1600	1600	1450
Practical Range S/A (m)	200	200	200	—[5]	—[5]	200
Practical Range Auto (m)	100	100	100	100	100	100
Rate of Fire (S/A (rpm))	40	40	40	—[5]	—[5]	40
Rate of Fire Auto (rpm)	100	100	100	100	100	100
Rate of Fire Cyclic (rpm)	900	800	900	700	650	900

Ammunition
Calibre   7·62mm[7]
Type   P
Round
Weight   170gr
Length   1·36in

Bullet   Weight 86gr
Propellant
Type   NCT[8]
Weight   8gr

1 Drum magazine
2 Box magazine

3 Stock extended
4 Stock retracted

5 Full auto only
6 North Vietnamese

7 Also takes 7·63mm Mauser
8 Tubular Nitro Cellulose

Heckler & Koch P9S Automatic Pistol. This is the double-action version of the P9 (*Heckler & Koch*)

Heckler & Koch—An Armoury

by A. J. R. Cormack

At the end of the Second World War the Germans were frantically searching for weapons which could overcome the lack of strategic materials and manufacturing facilities. It is out of these difficulties that some of the best and most advanced weapon development was carried out. After the war most of the design staffs of the German armament industries dispersed throughout Europe; some ended up in Spain, amongst whom was a former member of the Mauser Werke firm—Herr Volgrimmler. In Spain basic design concepts developed during the war were turned into drawings and then into production weapons at the Centro de Estudios Technicos de Materiales Especiales—in short CETME. This is a Government-run establishment to foster design and development work. These designs for a service rifle were later developed by Heckler & Koch. Thus from a very troubled childhood came a weapon type that was to equip a number of armed forces in a variety of guises.

The STG 45M Assault Rifle

During the latter part of the war, in 1945 a number of companies, of which Mauser was one, developed prototype assault rifles. These weapons all followed the same basic concept of a light selectable fire weapon, firing a short lower power cartridge than that normally employed in the standard service rifle, and as cheap in materials and as easy to construct as possible. The cartridge for which the weapons were chambered was the 7·92 short or Kurz. The 7·92mm by 33mm cartridge has a rimless bottlenecked case which was developed from the 7·92mm by 57mm Mauser service rifle round. Among the Mauser designers connected with the project were Dr Karl Meyer and Herr Altenberger who, together with Volgrimmler, developed a weapon using a delayed blowback system. This was only possible by the use of the comparatively low powered cartridge. The system used involved a twin roller lock which delayed the opening of the bolt until the pressure

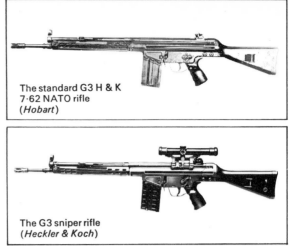

The standard G3 H & K
7·62 NATO rifle
(*Hobart*)

The G3 sniper rifle
(*Heckler & Koch*)

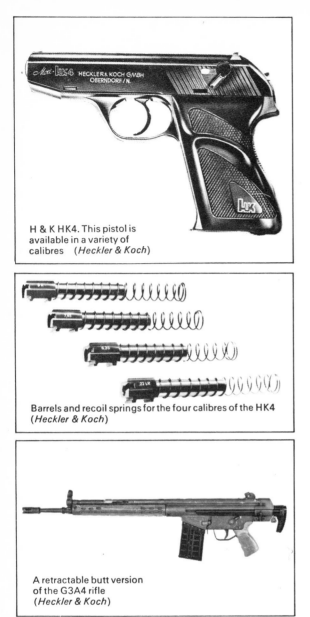

H & K HK4. This pistol is
available in a variety of
calibres   (*Heckler & Koch*)

Barrels and recoil springs for the four calibres of the HK4
(*Heckler & Koch*)

A retractable butt version
of the G3A4 rifle
(*Heckler & Koch*)

had dropped to a safe point. All blowback
weapons firing a high power cartridge suffer
from a basic problem stemming from the fact that
at the moment of firing some 50,000 psi pressure
holds the case against the walls of the chamber
and thus, unless some form of delay is used,
it is difficult for the extraction to take place
without the possibility of the case head being
ripped off and causing a total jam. Because of this
a fluted chamber was incorporated which, by
allowing the gases to float the front of the
cartridge case away from the chamber, eased the
initial extraction.

The above leads to the reputation of this type of
weapon being critical of the type of ammunition
used as cartridge cases which were either too
soft, or over-hard and brittle, led to immediate
head separation. The STG 45M weighed
8·18lbs and had an overall length of 35·15 inches
with a 15·75 inch barrel. A thirty-round detachable
box magazine was used and the Kurz cartridge
used gave a muzzle velocity of 2000+ ft/sec and
could be fired on full auto fire at a rate of
between 350 and 450 rpm. The lower power of the
round made the weapon easy to control on
full auto fire.

Close up of the Mauser developed roller lock assault
rifle   (*Pattern Room Enfield*)

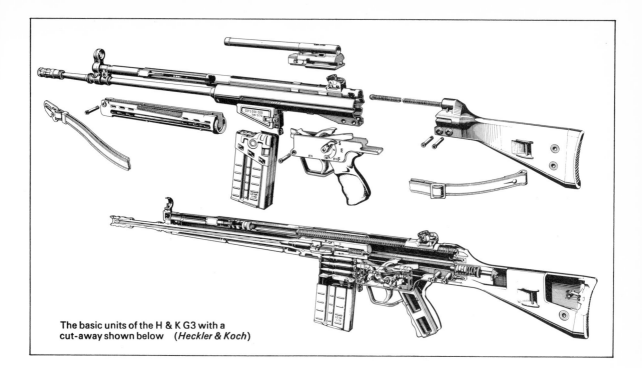

The basic units of the H & K G3 with a
cut-away shown below   (*Heckler & Koch*)

The weapon, which is well balanced, is
constructed from metal stampings and the extreme
simplicity of the design and the ease of
construction is evident although the practical
function remains unimpaired. After the war
Volgrimmler first went to France where he
developed a prototype carbine with delayed
blowback operation chambered for a short
7·65mm cartridge and then, after his work in
France, he moved on to Spain where he joined the
CETME organisation. The French model 52
machine gun uses the roller delayed blowback
operation which could have come from Volgrimmler
or possibly from the German machine gun of
the same type.

The CETME 7·62 Rifle

The CETME rifle is chambered for the 7·62mm
NATO round in its standard form although in its
original form in the early 1950's it was chambered
for the 7·92mm Kurz German cartridge then for a
special short 7·92mm cartridge. This cartridge
is of passing interest as the bullet was of
aluminium. Further development was carried out on
cartridge design and although finally
dimensionally, the NATO standard round was
adopted albeit with a reduced load, this means
that the standard NATO cartridge can only be used
with a different breech block. The 7·62 CETME
Model 58 has an overall length of 39·37 inches
with a barrel of 17·72 inches and a loaded weight
including a twenty round box magazine of
11·2 lbs. The fully auto fire cyclic rate of 600 rpm
and the velocity is 2540 fps in its lightly loaded
form as opposed to 2900fps in the NATO round.

Heckler & Koch

Heckler & Koch was founded in 1948 very close to
the old Mauser factory. This factory was

occupied on 20 April 1945 by the Free French
Army. For a short period the factory was kept in
production by the Allied Forces but at the
insistence of the Russians, as a reprisal against the
damage done to their own army by the munitions
produced in Oberndorf, it was razed to the
ground. Most of the inhabitants of the area
therefore, finding no work, spread throughout
Europe.

In 1948 Edmond Heckler, who had been a
plant manager during the war, Theodore Koch, a
manager at Mauser Werke, Alex Seidel a design
engineer at Mauser and an unamed financier
started a company to manufacture sewing machine
parts. By 1952 Heckler & Koch employed
250 people turning out sewing machine
components and parts and gauges for the tool
industry. One order which came their way was for
bolt components for the CETME rifle, followed
later by further contract work from CETME.
The West German Government after the war
equipped their armed forces with M1 rifles
purchased from the USA then purchased a number
of FN FAL 7·62 rifles and named them the G1. At
a later date the Government expressed interest
in the Spanish CETME and purchased a number.
The licensee for Europe for the CETME was
NWM who are based in the Netherlands and
under an agreement with the German
Government in 1954 they assigned this licence to
Heckler & Koch. Heckler & Koch then, between
1954 and 1956, developed the CETME rifle into
the G3 firing the full power NATO cartridge.
Eventually the weapon was accepted as a
standard service weapon for the German Army,
and by 1959 700,000 G3 rifles had been
supplied. The basic weapon has been a great
success and has been accepted by Norway,
Sweden, Denmark, Portugal and Pakistan amongst

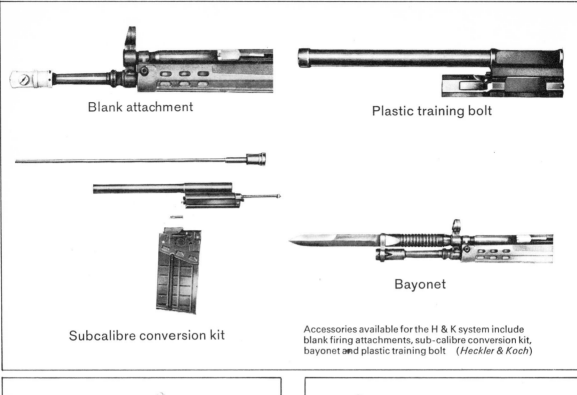

Blank attachment

Plastic training bolt

Subcalibre conversion kit

Bayonet

Accessories available for the H & K system include blank firing attachments, sub-calibre conversion kit, bayonet and plastic training bolt   (*Heckler & Koch*)

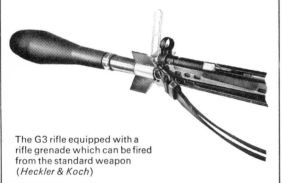

The G3 rifle equipped with a rifle grenade which can be fired from the standard weapon (*Heckler & Koch*)

The HK33 with the bipod centrally mounted (*Hobart*)

others. The basic delayed blowback roller-locking system has been developed into a complete range of weapons by Heckler & Koch ranging from a pistol to a machine gun and covering all weapons in between.

The factory from such small beginnings has grown to a concern with five factories and two thousand employees. Tragically in 1960 Edmond Heckler died leaving Theodore Koch and Alex Seidel to run the fast-expanding firm. Heckler & Koch is an interesting parallel to other German munitions factories in that initially the work carried out was not on weapons but on sewing machines (the Walther concern was another which initially did not manufacture weapons) until they were in a position to continue their true trade.

The Heckler & Koch armoury is divided into four parts: the three weapon groups and the pistols. These groups are built up as follows— Group One which is chambered for the NATO standard ammunition. That is the standard 7·62mm by 51mm NATO rifle round for the rifle, light machine gun and the machine gun, and the 9mm by 19mm parabellum round for the submachine gun.

Group Two consists of the same weapons; rifle, light machine gun, machine gun and submachine gun all chambered for the American ·223 Armalite 5·56mm by 45mm cartridge. This is itself is noteworthy as Heckler & Koch claim that the use of the rifle round for a submachine gun is only possible by the recoil reduction inherent in the roller lock system.

Group Three is the same as Group Two but is chambered for the Russian 7·62mm by 39mm cartridge. A submachine gun is not however offered. All these weapons use the same basic retarded blowback action and many parts are interchangeable from weapon to weapon. To show the basic strength and no doubt to dispel doubt about the delayed blowback operation Heckler & Koch also developed a ·50 calibre heavy machine gun. It weighed 36lbs; was

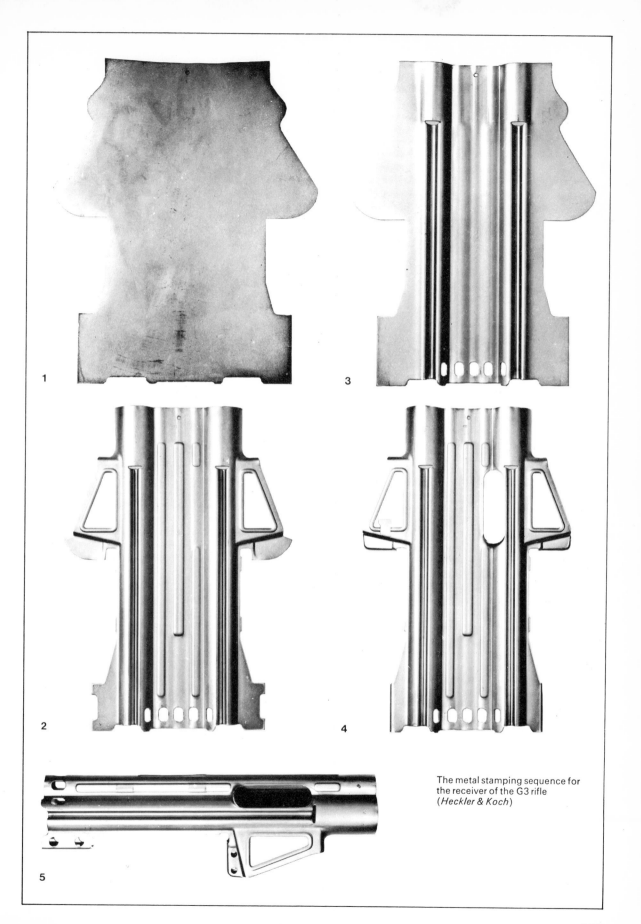

The metal stamping sequence for
the receiver of the G3 rifle
(*Heckler & Koch*)

Notice the short magazine on
this HK33 compared to the
previous illustration
(*Heckler & Koch*)

A breakdown of the
major components of the
HK33
(*Heckler & Koch*)

belt-fed and used the trigger group and butt stock
common to the system. This however is not
manufactured.

Lastly there are the pistols. These fall into two
categories—the P9 (the double action version of
the P9 is designated the P9S) which is a 9mm
parabellum pistol using the delayed blowback
roller lock system and the second the HK4
which is a straight blowback but chambered for a
selection of calibres ie ·22 Long Rifle, ·25 ACP,
·32 ACP and ·380 ACP, all calibres being
directly interchangeable.

H & K Automatic Pistol HK4

The HK4 pistol is the only weapon in the
Heckler & Koch armoury that does not feature the
roller operated delayed blowback system. This
pistol, which is a simple blowback with the
addition of a plastic buffer, has a number of
interesting features, the first of which is the choice
of four separate calibres, three centre fire and one
rim fire. This is accomplished by the use of
different barrels coupled with a moveable firing
pin. The second is the plastic buffer which helps to
absorb recoil. Heckler & Koch do acknowledge
the fact that the buffers wear and supply
spares with the gun. The four calibres are also
offered as a set; four barrels ·22 rim fire;
·25 ACP, ·32 ACP and ·380 ACP each with the

appropriate recoil spring and magazine.

The dimensions are as follows—6·18 inches long,
4·3 inches high with a barrel of 3·34 inches. The
pistol weighs 1·05lbs and the magazine
capacity varies with the calibre, ten in ·22 LR and
·25 ACP, nine in ·32 ACP and eight in ·380 ACP.
The other weapons in the Heckler & Koch
range are all of the retarded blowback system
which operates as follows: with the weapon in the
ready to fire position the bolt head and the
locking piece are forward behind the chambered
round; the locking piece forces the rollers
outwards into two recesses in the barrel
extension and thus prevents the bolt head from
movement when the weapon is fired. Because of
the carefully calculated angles of the locking
piece and the depth of the recesses the bolt
stays forward until the bullet has left the barrel. The
bolt head eventually overcomes the resistance

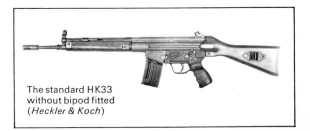

The standard HK33
without bipod fitted
(*Heckler & Koch*)

As with most weapons in the range a
sniper scope can be fitted to the HK33
(*Heckler & Koch*)

Two versions of the folding stock HK33K.
Notice the difference in barrel length and
size of the magazine   (*Heckler & Koch*)

and the locking piece is driven back thus
allowing the rollers out of the recesses and the
case, bolt head and assembly to move rearwards.
The empty case is ejected and then under the
influence of the recoil spring the bolt group
moves forward chambering a fresh round and
locking up the rollers.

The P9 and P9S Pistols
The P9 was designed by Herbert Midel using
the basic roller lock system but incorporating a
plastic recoil buffer. This weapon is full of
the most modern techniques of weapon
production using pressings extensively and
plastics wherever possible. Both the slide and the
basic frame are manufactured from pressings, the

frame is in two pieces, the slide a pressing with a
separate barrel bushing and block containing
the firing pin and attendant mechanism at the
rear. All the parts are welded together. As the
weapon has a concealed hammer Heckler &
Koch have fitted an indicator pin at the rear of the
slide which shows when a cartridge is in the
chamber. This is incorporated in the extractor in a
similar manner to the Luger. These features
provide the carrier with both visual indicators but,
more important, a touch indicator so that even
in the dark the firer can ascertain the
condition of the weapon.
The roller locking system combined with the
plastic buffer, which works on the last $\frac{3}{16}$ in of the
slide travel together give an unusually low recoil

The main components
shown field-stripped of
the HK33K
(*Heckler & Koch*)

The dual drum fitting on the HK11
(*Heckler & Koch*)

for a weapon chambering the 9mm parabellum round, making the weapon pleasant to fire. Apart from the other features incorporated, the rifling is the most unusual. Although the polygonal rifling is not new as it was used on the Metford rifle, and Heckler & Koch do not claim that it is, they do claim that this is the first time that it has been used without a considerable cost penalty. The claimed advantages are an increase in muzzle velocity, elimination of wear, and ease in cleaning. A considerable increase in service life and durability is brought about by the lack of sharp corners on the rifling. The plastic covering on the grip and frame gives good handling characteristics under extremes of both high and low temperatures.

The dimensions of the pistol are 5·4 inches long, 7·6 inches high with a barrel length of 4 inches. The pistol weighs 5·4 ounces and the magazine capacity is nine rounds.

H & K Group One Weapons

Group One contains the following—
The G3A3 and G3A4 automatic rifles, the HK11 light machine gun, the HK21 machine gun and the MP5A2 and MP5A3 submachine guns. All the weapons in Group One are chambered for standard NATO cartridges, the 7·62mm by 51mm cartridge for the rifles and machine guns and the universal 9mm by 19mm parabellum cartridge for the submachine guns.

Automatic Rifles G3A3 and G3A4

The G3 rifle development of the CETME is the basic weapon from which all others in the three groups are developed.
The G3 uses the roller-delayed lock and is capable of both semi-automatic fire and fully-automatic fire at a cyclic rate of between 500 and 600 rounds per minute fed from a twenty round box magazine. The weapon is hammer fired

and a recoil buffer is fitted which cushions the bolt at the rear of its travel and combined with the recoil spring returns the bolt forward. The weapon is mainly constructed from stampings making it cheap and easy to produce. The basic receiver unit takes some 19 stamping operations during its manufacture and although at first sight this seems complicated it must be remembered that in wartime the first tools to be needed are the machine tools, so that the ability to manufacture by stamping is very important. The hand guard and the buttstock are manufactured from plastic providing the essential of a comfortable grip in extremes of heat and cold. With the lack of a gas operating system such as used on some of the competitive weapons

there is no piston or 'plumbing' to become blocked under combat conditions.

The G3 is easy to maintain in that it is easy to field-strip and clean, an often overlooked matter—other weapons such as the AR15/M16 have had trouble from lack of cleaning. On the vital point of acceptability of different brands of ammunition it is said to be virtually insensitive and with the possibility of supply from different countries in NATO or acquisition from different sources in war, the importance of this cannot be emphasised enough.

As on most of the present generation of assault rifles, grenades can be launched from the basic weapon without any attachments. The German Army, as well as other forces, has adopted the G3

The HK13. Notice the front mounted bipod and drum magazine (*Heckler & Koch*)

The drum-equipped HK13 shown field-stripped (*Hobart*)

The cleaning rod and sight
adjustment tool for the H & K
system   (Hobart)

The adjustable rearsight fitted to the H & K range   (Hobart)

The foresight as fitted to the H & K range   (Hobart)

as their standard weapon; this can only be
accepted as the proof of the soundness of
the weapon.

The G3A4 is a version of the weapon using a
retractable stock thus making the weapon more
compact for the use of paratroops or tank crews.
The basic weapon breaks down into the
following main groups: the receiver with barrel and
roller operation mechanism; the grip with the
trigger assembly; the back plate and stock;
and the hand guard. These groups can, by
interchangeability, be used throughout the
weapon system thus simplifying both the spares
and production.

The G3 can be equipped with a blank firing
adaptor making the firing of blank cartridges on
semi- or fully-automatic fire possible. It is also
possible with the substitution of a plastic
practice bolt for practice firing to be done with a

form of plastic training ammunition. For
economic training a subcalibre attachment is
available for the firing of a 5·66mm subcalibre
ammunition. A sniper version which is equipped
with a telescopic sight is designated the G3A3ZF.
It is interesting to note the difference in weight
between the aluminium magazine which weighs
21·95 ounces filled, as compared to the steel
magazine which weighs 26·54 ounces filled. The
weight of the weapon with magazine is 8·66lbs.
As the G3 is the basic weapon in the system the
following additional information is given. The site
base is 22·48 inches, the rifling has four grooves
and one twist in 12 inches, the muzzle velocity of a
standard round is 2559 to 2624fps giving a
muzzle energy of 2098 to 2170ft/lbs. The
normal effective range is up to 437 yards while it
is indicative of the range of a standard round
that a safety limit in the direction of fire of some

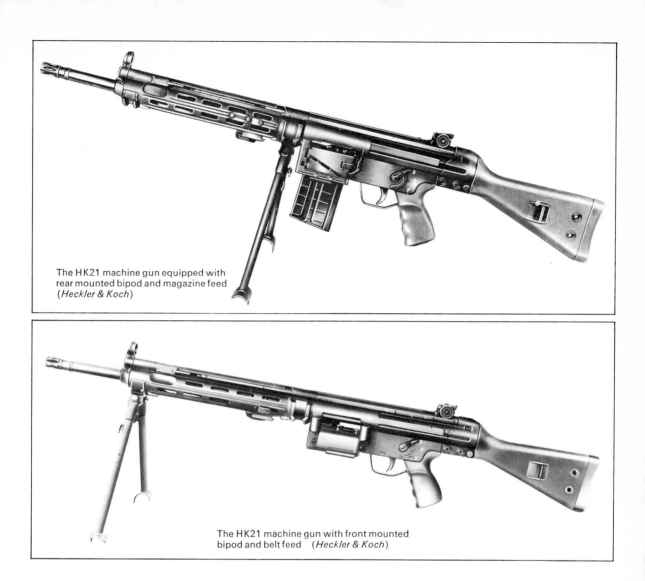

The HK21 machine gun equipped with
rear mounted bipod and magazine feed
(*Heckler & Koch*)

The HK21 machine gun with front mounted
bipod and belt feed   (*Heckler & Koch*)

4400 yards is required. A flash hider is fitted
which has a dual purpose of hiding the flash and
also acting as a guide for the fitting of the
rifle grenade. This flash hider is removeable for the
fitting of the different muzzle attachments. The rear
sight is of a rotary type giving a sight position
for each of 100, 200, 300 and 400 metres. An
infra-red night sight device is available
comprising a projector unit and a telescope. This
enables accurate fire to be maintained in total
darkness. The chamber has twelve grooves
in it to assist in initial extraction. The
dimensions of the weapons are :
G3A3—40·15 inches long : G3A4—stock extended
40·15 inches : stock folded 31·49 inches. The
barrel length on both weapons is 17·71 inches
and the weight of the G3A3 is 9·37lbs and the
G3A4 9·93lbs.

The Light Machine Gun HK11
The HK11 is a basic derivative of the G3 rifle
and has been developed as a general purpose light
machine gun (GPMG). It utilises the same
basic groups of components as the G3 but offers
the choice of a 30 round box magazine or an 80

round double drum magazine and the capability
of both semi- and fully-automatic fire by the use of
a heavy barrel. The HK11 is normally equipped
with a front mounted bipod when fitted with the
drum magazine and a centre mounted one if
the box magazine is in use. The HK11 is of a
selective fire nature and once again a full range of
accessories is offered. The dimensions are
40·15 inches long, barrel length of 17·71 inches,
weight without magazine and bipod of 13·70lbs.
The bipod weighs 1·32lbs.

The HK21 Machine Gun
This weapon differs from the HK11 in that
although the barrel is basically fixed it is
interchangeable and thus more suitable than the
former for a sustained fire role. The standard feed
utilises metal link belts and is so designed
that both disintegrating and joined types can be
used. As with the other weapon there are many of
the groups that are interchangeable with the
basic G3. The weapon can be used with the bipod
in either position or alternatively for sustained
fire with the tripod designed by Heckler & Koch.
The weapon is selective fire and on fully-

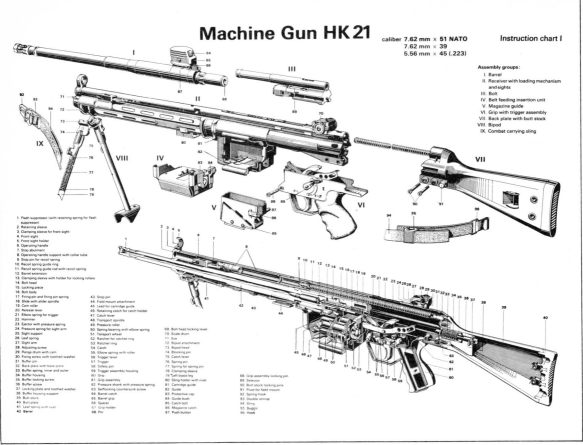

A cutaway view and major component breakdown of the HK21
(*Heckler & Koch*)

automatic will fire at approximately 850 rounds per minute.

The dimensions are 40·15 inches long with a barrel length of 17·71 inches and a weight with bipod of 16·10lbs. A spare barrel weighs 3·75lbs.

The MP5 Submachine Gun

This weapon which was adopted by the police forces of the German Republic in the autumn of 1966 and by the Federal German Border Police soon after, has the basic roller lock system. It is chambered for the almost standard 9mm parabellum cartridge and is of a selective fire type. The cartridges are contained in a 30 round box magazine and as the MP5 fires from a closed bolt position unlike the majority of submachine guns it is very accurate. The closed bolt position type of firing is usually avoided on fully automatic weapons as there is a danger of a chambered round 'cooking off'. The term is self-descriptive as the round fires itself as the result of 'cooking' by the residual heat in the chamber. The open bolt position allows the chamber to cool off between bursts. Heckler & Koch are adamant that their weapons do not suffer from this problem. Once again the main construction is from metal stampings. The weapon

is available in two versions, the MP5A2 which has a fixed stock and the MP5A3 with a retractable one.

The dimensions of the weapons are—MP5A2 26·77 inches; MP5A3 butt retracted 19·29 inches extended 26·00 inches; barrel length 8·85 inches. The MP5A2 weighs 5·4lbs and the MP5A3 5·6lbs. The rate of fire is approximately 650rpm.

The Heckler & Koch Weapons System Group II

This group comprises a rifle, light machine gun, machine gun and a submachine gun all chambered for the 5·56mm by 45mm ·223 cartridge.

The HK33 Rifle and the HK33K Carbine

This rifle is very similar to the G3 but being chambered for the less powerful ·223 round the construction is lighter. The HK33 fires from the closed bolt position on either single or fully automatic fire and is fed from either 20 or 40 round box magazines. Once again the weapon can fire rifle grenades, be fitted with a bipod or a bayonet, and have a telescopic sight. For the use of paratroops or vehicle crews the HK33 can have a folding stock or under the designation

HK33K be issued as an assault rifle or carbine with a shorter barrel and folding stock standard. This version is not however capable of firing rifle grenades.

The HK53 Submachine Gun
The HK53 is possibly unique as a submachine gun in that it has been designed to fire ·223 rifle

The dimensions are

	HK33	HK33K
Length of Stock folded	29·52 ins	26·37 ins
Length of Stock open	36·22 ins	34·05 ins
Length of Fixed Stock	36·22 ins	
Barrel length	15·35 ins	12·67 ins
Weight—Fixed Stock	7·38 lbs	
Weight—Folding Stock	7·60 lbs	8·16 lbs
Magazine weight 20 round	4·05 ozs	
Magazine weight 40 round	5·65 ozs	

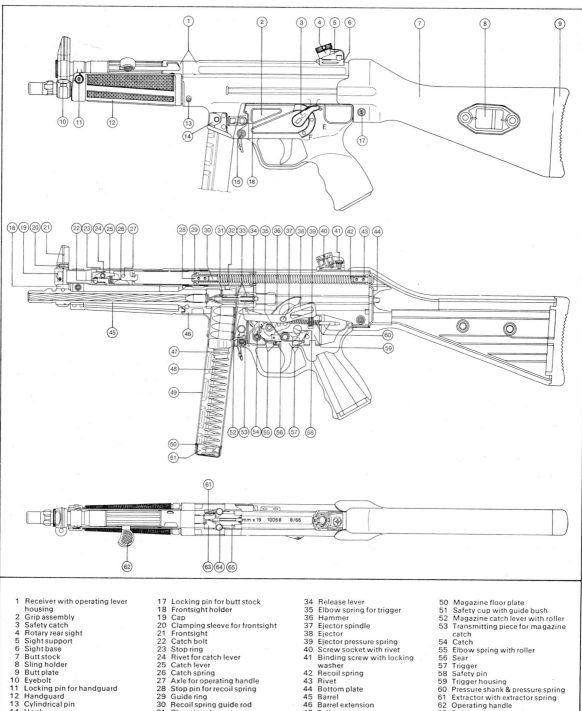

1 Receiver with operating lever housing	17 Locking pin for butt stock	34 Release lever	50 Magazine floor plate
2 Grip assembly	18 Frontsight holder	35 Elbow spring for trigger	51 Safety cup with guide bush
3 Safety catch	19 Cap	36 Hammer	52 Magazine catch lever with roller
4 Rotary rear sight	20 Clamping sleeve for frontsight	37 Ejector spindle	53 Transmitting piece for magazine catch
5 Sight support	21 Frontsight	38 Ejector	54 Catch
6 Sight base	22 Catch bolt	39 Ejector pressure spring	55 Elbow spring with roller
7 Butt stock	23 Stop ring	40 Screw socket with rivet	56 Sear
8 Sling holder	24 Rivet for catch lever	41 Binding screw with locking washer	57 Trigger
9 Butt plate	25 Catch lever	42 Recoil spring	58 Safety pin
10 Eyebolt	26 Catch spring	43 Rivet	59 Trigger housing
11 Locking pin for handguard	27 Axle for operating handle	44 Bottom plate	60 Pressure shank & pressure spring
12 Handguard	28 Stop pin for recoil spring	45 Barrel	61 Extractor with extractor spring
13 Cylindrical pin	29 Guide ring	46 Barrel extension	62 Operating handle
14 Hook	30 Recoil spring guide rod	47 Follower	63 Bolt head
15 Locking pin for grip assembly	31 Clamping sleeve	48 Follower spring	64 Locking roller
16 Magazine catch	32 Bolt body	49 Magazine tube	65 Locking piece
	33 Firing pin with firing pin spring		

The HK21 fitted on a tripod with
special sighting gear and belt feed
(This is for a sustained fire role)
(*Heckler & Koch*)

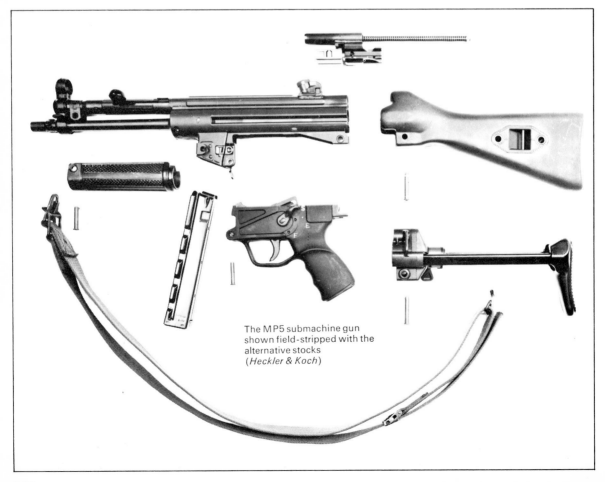

The MP5 submachine gun
shown field-stripped with the
alternative stocks
(*Heckler & Koch*)

Left side of MP5 with folding stock
(*Heckler & Koch*)

Cutaway of the 9mm P9 pistol
(*Heckler & Koch*)

Comparative view of conventional rifling
groove design versus polygonal groove
design   (*Heckler & Koch*)

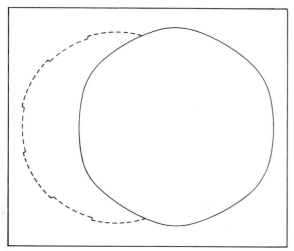

cartridges. It utilises the same basic concepts as
the other weapons in the Heckler & Koch
system using the delayed blowback operation
with the roller lock. It is a selective fire weapon,
single or burst fire being possible, fed from a 40
round box magazine. A retractable butt stock
is fitted as standard but a rigid butt stock can be
had as an option. The basic dimensions are
as follows: length with retractable butt stock
retracted 22 inches; butt stock extended
30·11 inches; barrel 8·85 inches; weapon weighs
without magazine 7·40lbs; magazine made of
aluminium 5·65 ounces. It has a cycle rate of fire of
600 rounds per minute.

HK13 Light Machine Gun
This weapon is similar to the HK11 Light
Machine gun in that the accessories are identical
as is the method of operation. The magazine
types are the same except that the dual drum
magazine contains 100 rounds and the box
magazine 40 rounds (a 20-round box magazine is
also available.) The HK13 fires at a rate of
800rpm when fully-automatic fire is selected. The
dimensions which are interesting to compare
with those of the HK11 are: length 38·6 inches;
barrel 17·7 inches; weight 11·68lbs; barrel
weight 3·75lbs.

HK21 Machine Gun
This weapon is identical in all three groups
apart from the barrel, belt feed insert and the
bolt. For full details refer to the 7·62 NATO HK11.

The Group III Weapon System
This group is chambered for the 7·62mm by 39mm
Soviet cartridge and consists of a rifle HK32,
light machine gun HK12 and the machine gun
HK21. These weapons are identical to those in
Group II and therefore no separate description is
necessary. The weapons are available with

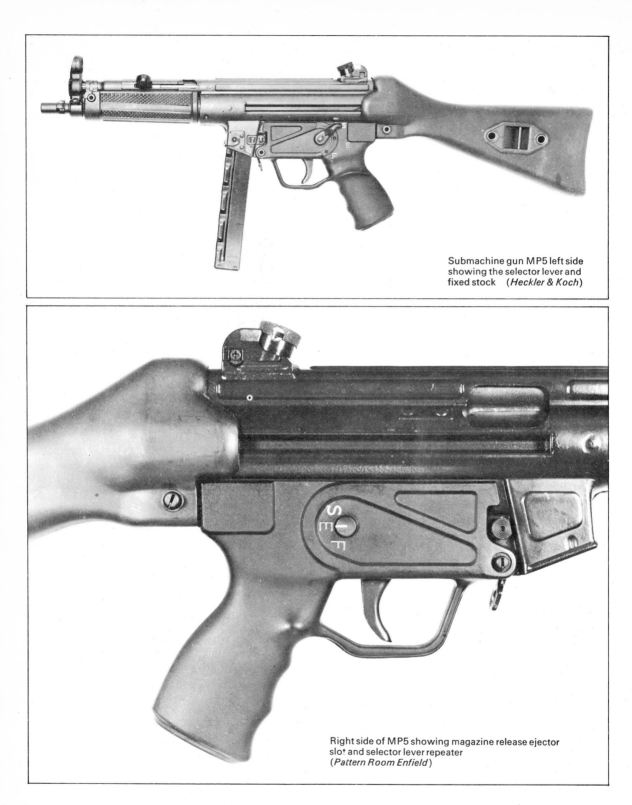

Submachine gun MP5 left side showing the selector lever and fixed stock   (*Heckler & Koch*)

Right side of MP5 showing magazine release ejector slot and selector lever repeater (*Pattern Room Enfield*)

the standard accessories and attachments common to the range.

The Heckler & Koch weapon systems must rate very high in the competitive field of small arms as they have been accepted by the Bundeswehr as standard equipment in at least two forms. The basic G3 has been used in combat and proved efficient. The basis of a weapon system with the interchangeability and thus the easing of the replacement of both parts and weapons coupled with the cheapness brought about by the use of stampings must make it worthy of consideration by any power equipping their army. Above all the system allows the choice to suit any given combat situation and is thus ideal for the present-day type of guerilla warfare.

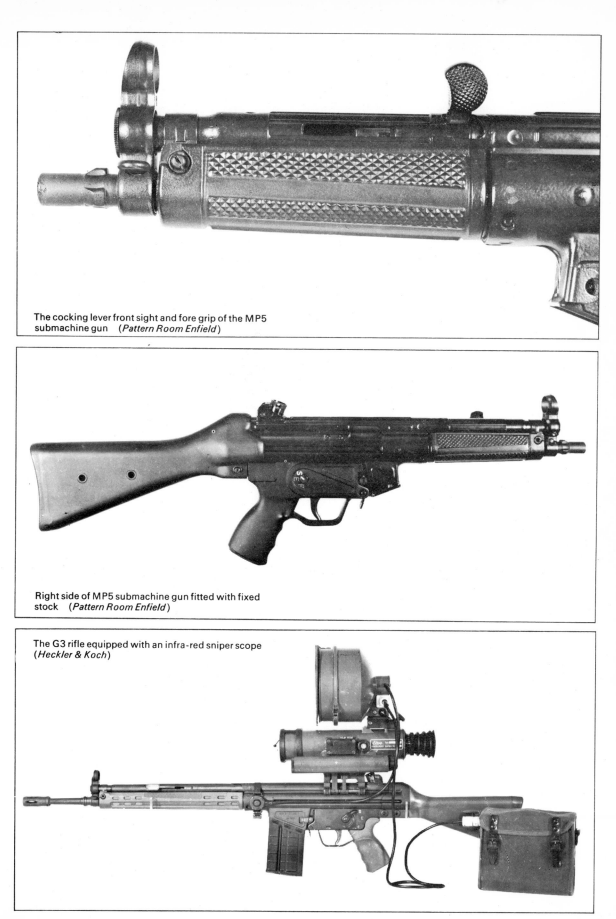

The cocking lever front sight and fore grip of the MP5 submachine gun   (*Pattern Room Enfield*)

Right side of MP5 submachine gun fitted with fixed stock   (*Pattern Room Enfield*)

The G3 rifle equipped with an infra-red sniper scope (*Heckler & Koch*)

Left side of the Mauser prototype STG45M assault rifle
(*Pattern Room Enfield*)

The prototype STG45M assault rifle manufactured by
Mauser in the closing stages of World War II
(*Pattern Room Enfield*)

This illustration shows the number of components that go to
make the modern service weapon   (*Heckler & Koch*)

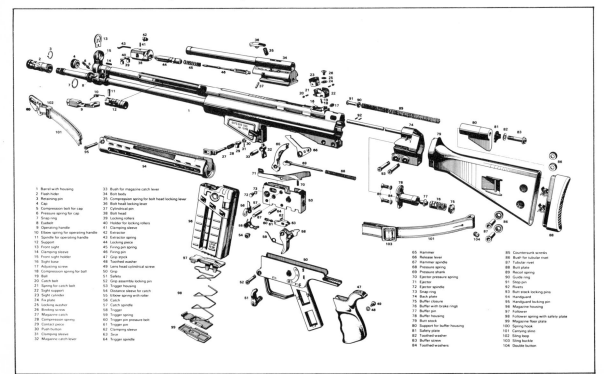

1 Barrel with housing
2 Flash hider
3 Retaining pin
4 Cap
5 Compression bolt for cap
6 Pressure spring for cap
7 Snap ring
8 Eyebolt
9 Operating handle
10 Elbow spring for operating handle
11 Spindle for operating handle
12 Support
13 Front sight
14 Clamping sleeve
15 Front sight holder
16 Sight base
17 Adjusting screw
18 Compression spring for ball
19 Ball
20 Catch bolt
21 Spring for catch bolt
22 Sight support
23 Sight cylinder
24 Fix plate
25 Locking washer
26 Binding screw
27 Magazine catch
28 Compression spring
29 Contact piece
30 Push button
31 Clamping sleeve
32 Magazine catch lever

33 Bush for magazine catch lever
34 Bolt body
35 Compression spring for bolt head locking lever
36 Bolt head locking lever
37 Cylindrical pin
38 Bolt head
39 Locking rollers
40 Holder for locking rollers
41 Clamping sleeve
42 Extractor
43 Extractor spring
44 Locking piece
45 Firing pin spring
46 Firing pin
47 Grip stock
48 Toothed washer
49 Lens head cylindrical screw
50 Grip
51 Safety
52 Grip assembly locking pin
53 Trigger housing
54 Distance sleeve for catch
55 Elbow spring with roller
56 Catch
57 Catch spindle
58 Trigger
59 Trigger spring
60 Trigger pin pressure bolt
61 Trigger pin
62 Clamping sleeve
63 Sear
64 Trigger spindle

65 Hammer
66 Release lever
67 Hammer spindle
68 Pressure spring
69 Pressure shank
70 Ejector pressure spring
71 Ejector
72 Ejector spindle
73 Snap ring
74 Back plate
75 Buffer closure
76 Buffer with brake rings
77 Buffer pin
78 Buffer housing
79 Butt stock
80 Support for buffer housing
81 Safety plate
82 Toothed washer
83 Buffer screw
84 Toothed washers

85 Countersunk screws
86 Bush for tubular rivet
87 Tubular rivet
88 Butt plate
89 Recoil spring
90 Guide ring
91 Stop pin
92 Rivets
93 Butt stock locking pins
94 Handguard
95 Handguard locking pin
96 Magazine housing
97 Follower
98 Follower spring with safety plate
99 Magazine floor plate
100 Spring hook
101 Carrying sling
102 Sling loop
103 Sling buckle
104 Double button

Troops equipped with a SIG W5-7 crossing barbed wire barricade   (*SIG*)

The SIG Service Rifle

by A. J. R. Cormack

The development of the military rifle in the 19th century was continually under the shadow of Prussia's success with the all-conquering Dreyse Needle Fire Rifle. The result was the almost panic stricken attempts to find an efficient alternative to it. On 17 January 1853 the firm of 'Swiss Railway Carriage Factory' near Schaffhausen was formed by three businessmen—Friedrich Peyer im Hof, Heinrich Moser and Colonel Conrad Neher. The factory employed 150 people and was situated on the edge of the Rhine Falls so that electrical power could be generated from the Falls. Even today the Falls supply the complete electric needs of the factory—some 4600 kilowatts and also provides the factory with one of the most picturesque settings imaginable. As its name suggests, the factory initially produced railway carriages which even today are one of the major products of the factory.

Prelaz Burnard

In 1860 Colonel Burnard became the first Director of Arms at the factory and, in conjunction with a gunsmith, started the Swiss Railway Carriage Factory on its way in weapon production. Prelaz, an experienced gunsmith, brought with him the details for rifling gun barrels and with help of Colonel Burnard started the production of a rifled weapon named after them.

In 1863 the factory was renamed the Schweizerische Industrie Gesellschaft, or the Swiss Industrial Company. This name has been shortened to the initials SIG for everyday usage and it is under these that they are best known today.

Vettereli 1869-1881

In 1864 Friedrich Vettereli became the Director of the SIG Small Arms Factory, a position that he was to retain until 1882. During this time he was the technical designer of a repeating rifle which was produced in prototype form in 1867. The weapon went into production in 1868 after some initial teething troubles, and was adopted by the Swiss Army in 1869 as their ordnance or standard weapon. The Swiss Government weapon factory, Waffenfabrik of Bern, also manufactured the Vettereli as well as developing a number of different versions of it.

The Vettereli rifle was a turn bolt weapon with the

locking lugs at the rear and with a tube magazine. The use of the tube magazine is explained by the use of a similar type on the American Winchester and Henry. Vertical Box Magazines were not invented until 1886 and even the first Mauser had a tube. The feed mechanism owed a lot to the Model 1866 Winchester, utilising a lifting cage to carry the cartridge from the magazine to the breech. The tube magazine carried twelve cartridges and was loaded through a side gate in a similar manner to the Winchester, although on the Vettereli the gate was covered by a swinging cover. The copper-cased cartridge was a rimfire known variously as the 10·2 Vettereli, the ·41 Swiss, or the 10·4 by 38, which used a 313 grain bullet and had a muzzle velocity of 1427fps.

The SIG factory continued to diversify and in 1906 entered the field of packing machinery. At first glance this might seem an odd choice, but it must be remembered that SIG are, above all things, expert engineers.

When the Swiss decided to adopt the Service Rifle designed by Colonel Schmidt and Lieutenant-Colonel Rubin at the State Ordnance Factory at Bern where Schmidt was the Director, SIG were asked to produce some of the parts. The Model 1889 Schmidt-Rubins was adopted as the Ordnance Weapon of the Swiss Army in 1889 and SIG manufactured receivers, barrels, butt stocks and hand guards. SIG did not (at any time) manufacture the complete weapons only the above components. A modification of the Model 1889 was however developed by them.

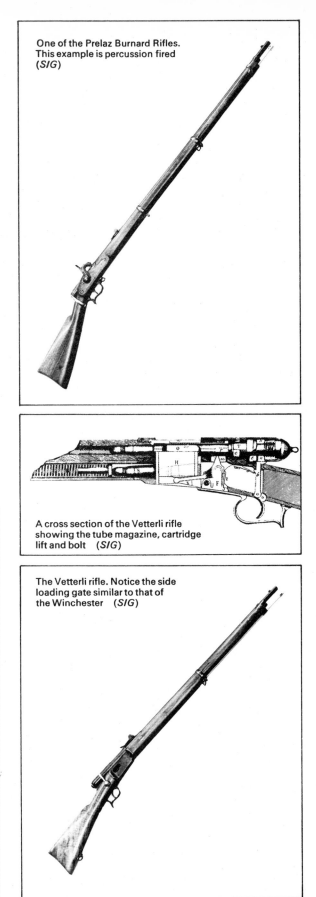

One of the Prelaz Burnard Rifles. This example is percussion fired (*SIG*)

A cross section of the Vetterli rifle showing the tube magazine, cartridge lift and bolt (*SIG*)

The Vetterli rifle. Notice the side loading gate similar to that of the Winchester (*SIG*)

The first Arms Director of the SIG Factory—Friedrich Vetterli (*SIG*)

The SIG Factory. In front the Falls of the Rhine with just behind the buildings of the SIG factory. In the middle Neuhausen and in the background Schaffhausen (*SIG*)

Mondragon

At the turn of the century SIG were still looking for a design for a service rifle that would be an advance on the bolt action Schmidt-Rubin and thus were attracted to the design of the Mexican General Manuel Mondragon. In 1908 SIG started to develop the weapon and in 1911 to produce it. During the First World War the Germans decided that they would use the weapon and thus it became the first gas operated weapon to see active service.

The Germans found out, however, that the weapon was not a combat one in that it became unreliable when used in muddy and rigorous trench warfare. They did, however, use it in limited numbers from their aircraft. Hence they called it the Aircraft Self Loading Carbine Model 1915.

The operation of the Mondragon utilised a gas port at the muzzle of the weapon that bled off gas to operate a piston that in turn unlocked the breech. The weapon had a ten-round box magazine and although it was not a combat success it was manufactured to the usual high standard that typifies SIG weapons. The failure of the weapons led the Swiss Army to utilise the Schmidt-Rubins until the end of the Second World War albeit in a number of different models and with improvements in the ammunition. However, the success of the German First World War Automatic Rifles had not escaped them and at the end of the war the SIG concern and the Government Weapon Factory began extensive development work into the design of a new weapon for the Swiss Army.

KE Series

During the period between 1924 and 1929 a number of self loading carbines were designed. These were all recoil operated and the final one in the series was the KE9. These weapons were not adopted by the Army and so development continued. One of the KE series to achieve production was the KE7 Light Machine Gun which was a light-weight selective fire weapon that fired from an open bolt. This was sold to China in small quantities. The shape of the weapon and its light weight of only 17lbs makes it similar in appearance to the earlier automatic rifles. At the same time the Factory continued to carry out contract work for the Federal Weapons Factory and made the main component parts for the Furrer Light Machine Gun, (eventually replaced by the SIG STgw 57).

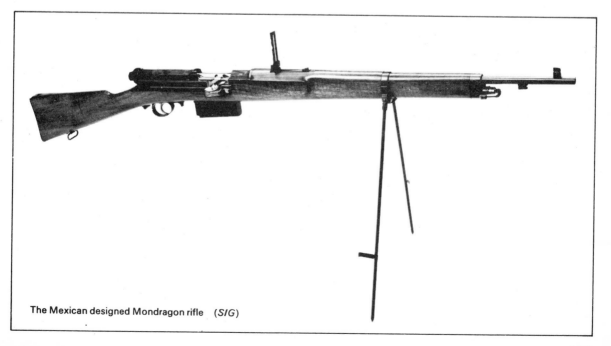

The Mexican designed Mondragon rifle (*SIG*)

KEG and N Series

The KEG series of weapons named Models A, B, C and D were all gas operated and the initials stand for the designers Kiraly, End and Gaetzi. All the weapons were made only in prototype self-loading carbine form between 1930 and 1932. The Series N42 to N46 were developed in 1942-46 and utilised a gas port connected by a long tube to the combined gas piston and breech. Once more the N series weapons were only produced in prototype form. Unfortunately SIG have very little information on the KE, KEG and N Series weapons.

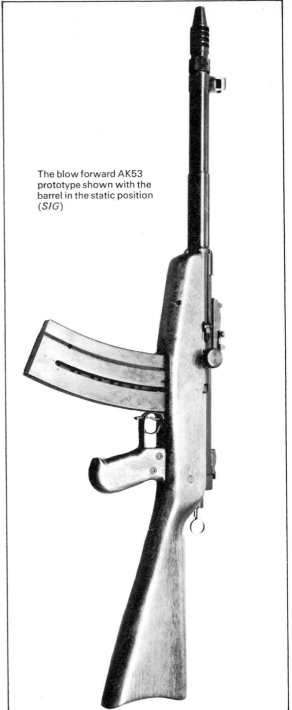

The blow forward AK53 prototype shown with the barrel in the static position (*SIG*)

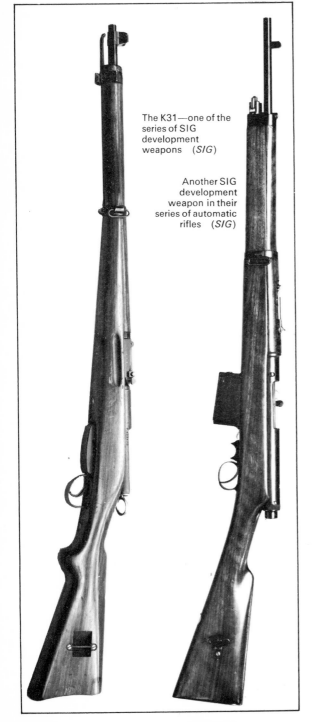

The K31—one of the series of SIG development weapons (*SIG*)

Another SIG development weapon in their series of automatic rifles (*SIG*)

SK46

Under the direction of Rudolf Amsler, SIG continued to develop prototype weapons which, with those developed by the Federal Weapons Factory, competed for the replacement of the Schmidt-Rubins.

The first SIG prototype developed in 1946 was the SK46 which was similar in outward appearance to the standard Rubins bolt action weapon, but featured a short gas-operating system. The gas, which was bled off very close to the chamber, operated a piston which was at the side of the

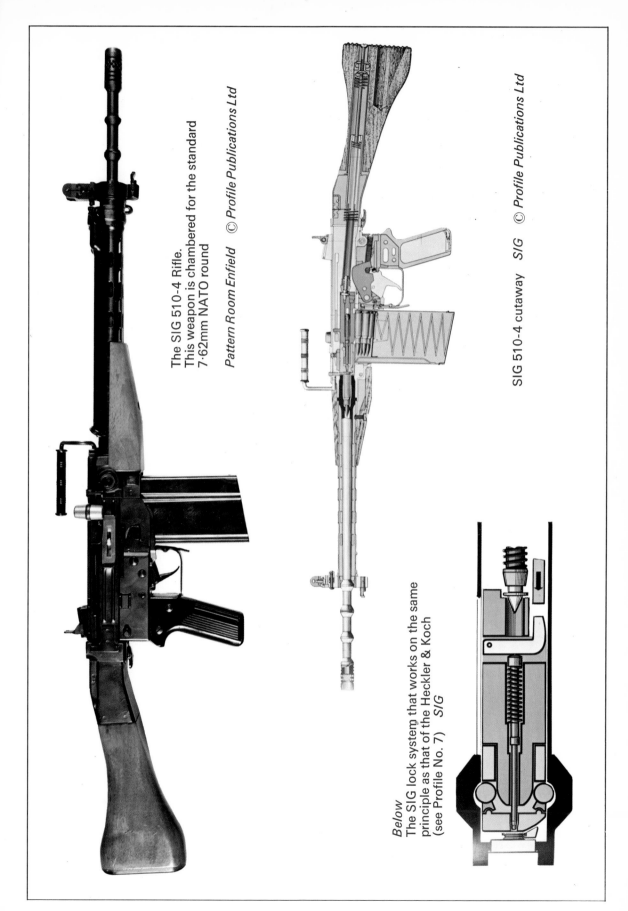

The SIG 510-4 Rifle.
This weapon is chambered for the standard
7·62mm NATO round

Pattern Room Enfield © *Profile Publications Ltd*

SIG 510-4 cutaway   *SIG*   © *Profile Publications Ltd*

Below
The SIG lock system that works on the same
principle as that of the Heckler & Koch
(see Profile No. 7)   *SIG*

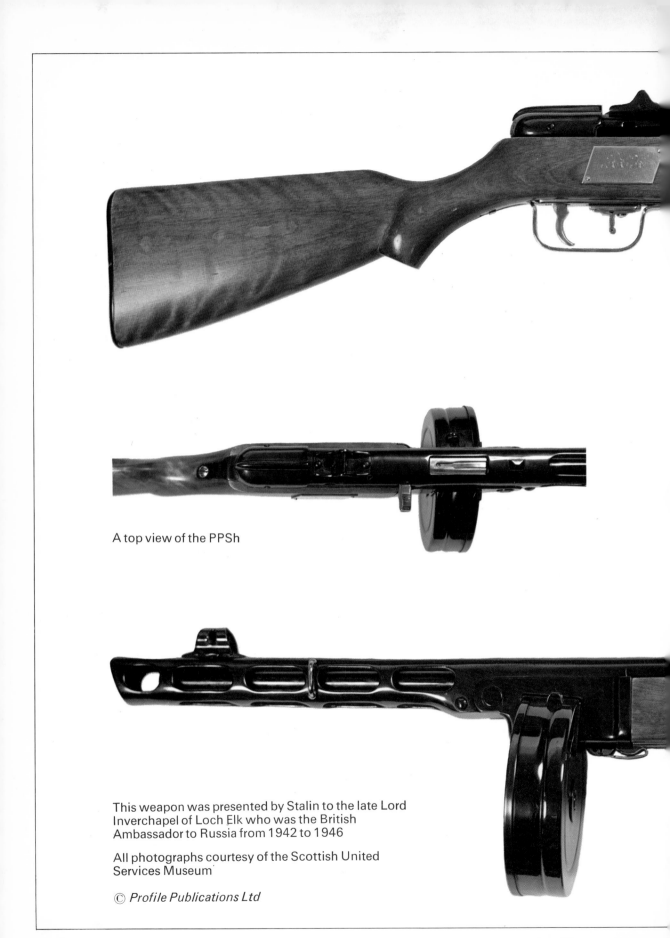

A top view of the PPSh

This weapon was presented by Stalin to the late Lord Inverchapel of Loch Elk who was the British Ambassador to Russia from 1942 to 1946

All photographs courtesy of the Scottish United Services Museum

© Profile Publications Ltd

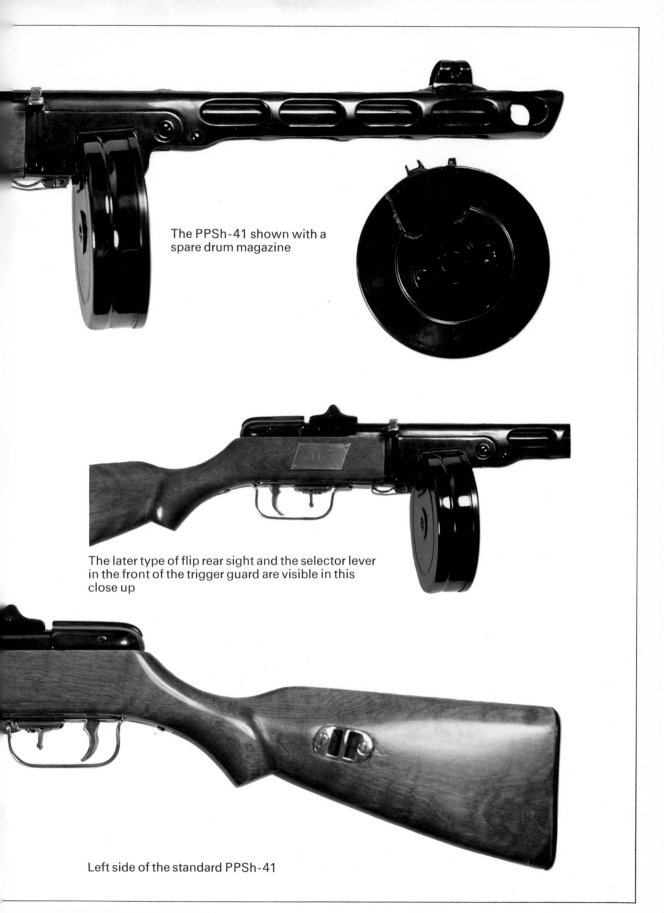

The PPSh-41 shown with a
spare drum magazine

The later type of flip rear sight and the selector lever
in the front of the trigger guard are visible in this
close up

Left side of the standard PPSh-41

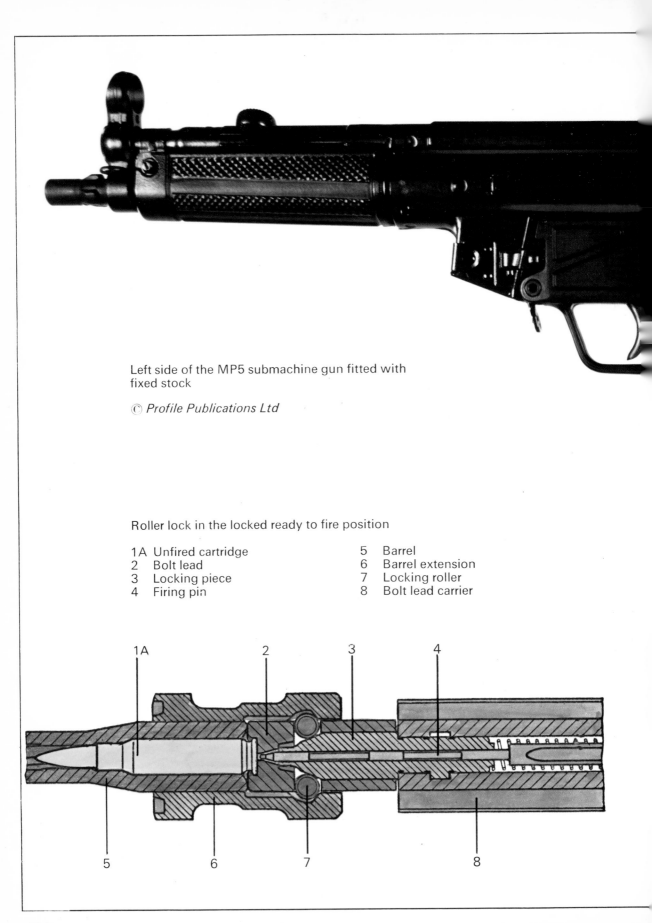

Left side of the MP5 submachine gun fitted with
fixed stock

© *Profile Publications Ltd*

Roller lock in the locked ready to fire position

1A	Unfired cartridge	5	Barrel
2	Bolt lead	6	Barrel extension
3	Locking piece	7	Locking roller
4	Firing pin	8	Bolt lead carrier

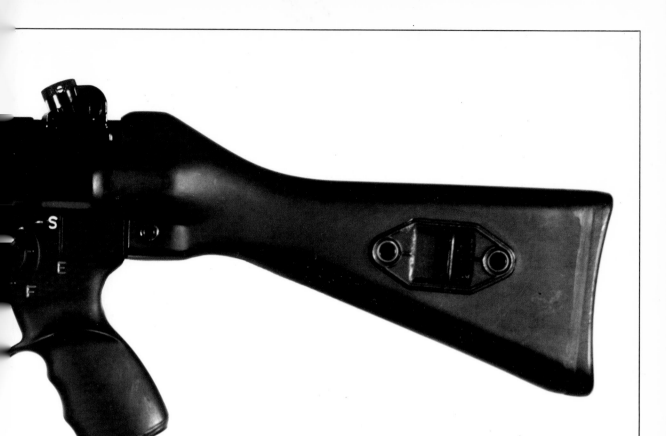

Roller lock unlocked at the start of the ejection cycle

1B Fired cartridge case
9   Fluted chamber
10 Locking recess

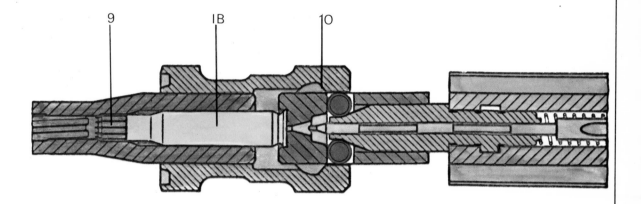

© Profile Publications Ltd

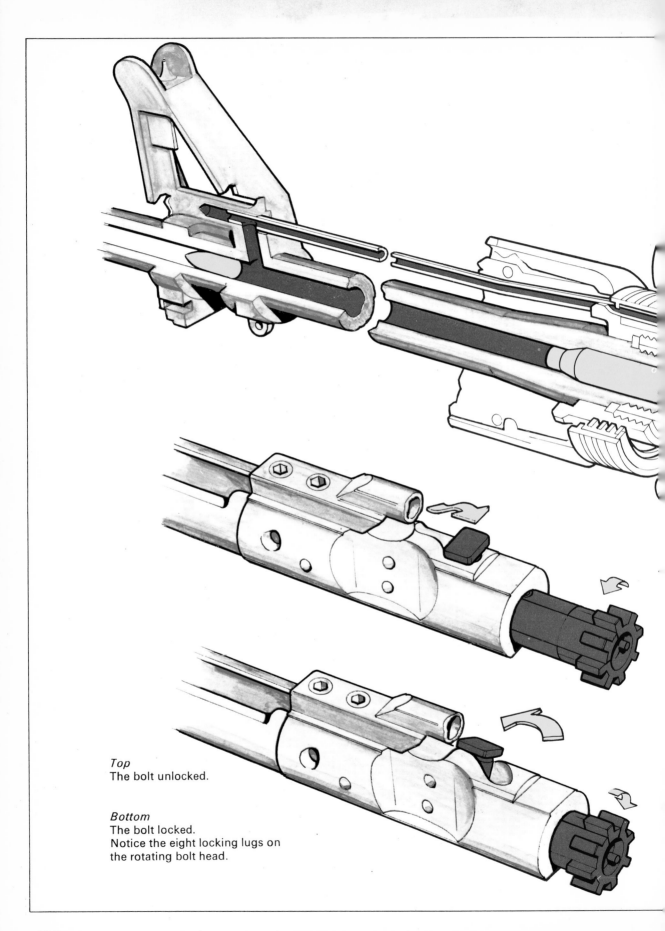

Top
The bolt unlocked.

Bottom
The bolt locked.
Notice the eight locking lugs on
the rotating bolt head.

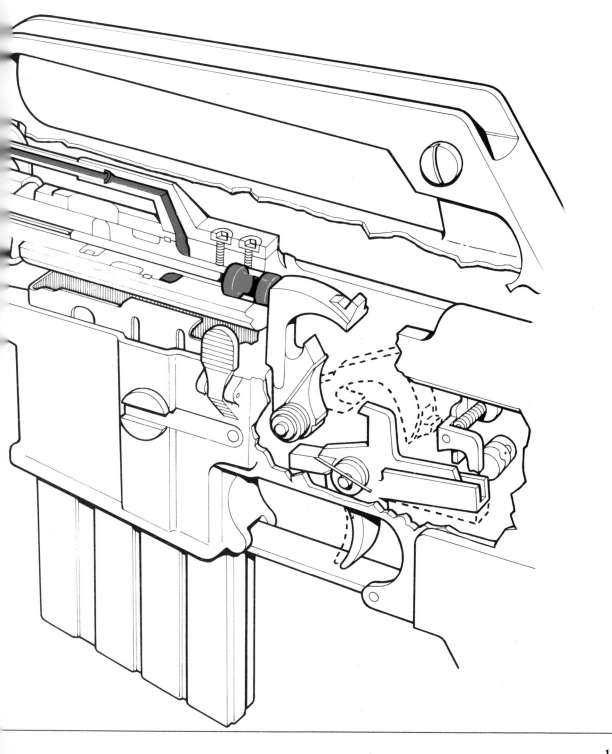

The Armalite AR15 (M16) Rifle.

The Stoner designed direct gas system is shown immediately after
firing but before the breech has unlocked.

T. Brittain © Profile Publications Ltd.

The Automat Karabine 53 or AK53.
This weapon features a blowforward action

Pattern Room Enfield © *Profile Publications Ltd*

The AK53 with the barrel blown forward. Notice that the cocking lever is also forward and the breech is open (*SIG*)

Left side of a further development of the AK53. Notice the ribbed barrel jacket (*Pattern Room Enfield*)

receiver. This moved the tilting locking bolt out of a groove in the top of the receiver, allowing the action to move back ejecting the spent case and on its spring assisted forward movement chamber a live round.

AK53—Automat Karabine

The next development was in 1953 and was called the Automat Karabine 53 or AK53 of which some fifty were made for Government trial. This weapon was truly remarkable as it featured a system that saw little or no use and had no success. This is the blow-forward system, in this particular application

An AK53 fitted with a front mounted bipod. The weapon is 1000mm long with a barrel length of 600mm and weighs 4·9kg   (*SIG*)

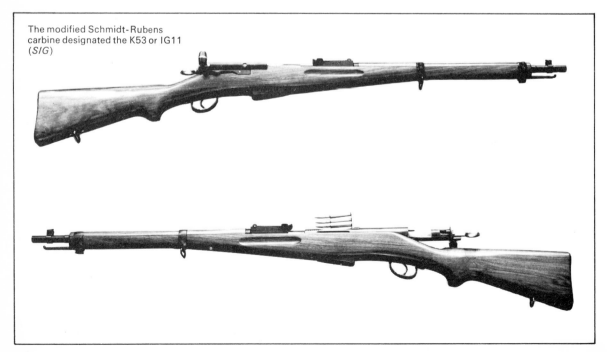

The KE7 Light Machine Gun.
Notice the similarity in concept
between this weapon and the
BAR   (*SIG*)

The modified Schmidt-Rubens
carbine designated the K53 or IG11
(*SIG*)

with a breech lock. In this system, as the name indicates, the barrel is blown forward by the firing of the cartridge. The gas piston drives the barrel forward, assisted by a spring leaving the empty case to be ejected by an ejector attached to the barrel. The barrel is returned by a second spring stripping a fresh round from the box magazine and chambering it. This system allowed a very low rate of fire, some 300 rpm and therefore no need for a single shot capability, as with a little practice the trigger could be used to fire single rounds. This weapon is chambered for the Swiss 7·5mm Model 11 cartridge as was the SK46.

AM55
The last series of weapons was finalised in 1955 and utilised lessons learned from the previous series, and from the German STG45 assault rifle. This weapon, chambered for the 7·5mm Swiss Model II

cartridge was adopted by the army in 1957 to replace the venerable Schmidt-Rubin. The Swiss Army designation for the weapon is the StGw57. The standard rifle can be fired either semi- or fully-automatically and with a bipod fitted it can fulfil some of the roles of a light machine gun. With no extra fittings or accessories both anti-tank and anti-personnel grenades can be fired at both high and low trajectories. A special device allowing the firing of a standard blank cartridge is available and a bayonet can be fitted. The weapon is light in weight and considering the use of a full-power cartridge the

The self loading SK46 rifle developed by SIG. The weapon here is fitted with a telescopic sight   (*SIG*)

The SK46 (Selbselade Karabiner). This SIG developed self loading rifle is designed to fire single shots only. It is 1125mm long, the barrel length is 600mm and weighs 4·5kg (*SIG*)

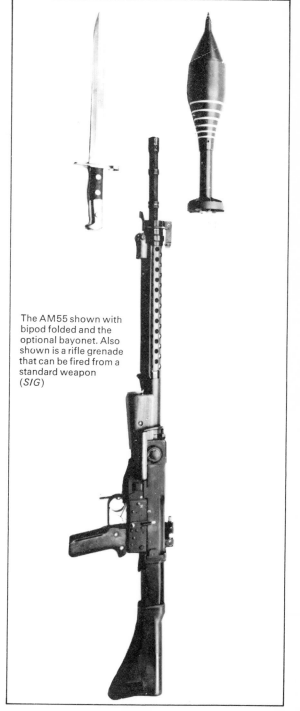

The AM55 shown with bipod folded and the optional bayonet. Also shown is a rifle grenade that can be fired from a standard weapon (*SIG*)

The SIG AM55 self loading rifle shown fitted with a bipod.
This is a prototype weapon   (*SIG*)

The AM55 left side showing the selector lever, carrying
handle and bipod   (*SIG*)

The Swiss Ordnance Weapon StGw57—a development
of the AM55   (*SIG*)

StGw57 shown with the bipod folded.
Notice the selector lever and carrying
handle   (*SIG*)

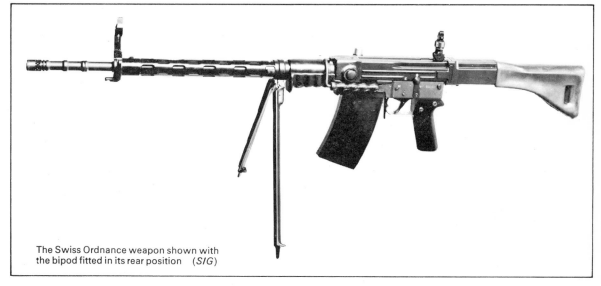

The Swiss Ordnance weapon shown with
the bipod fitted in its rear position   (*SIG*)

locking system similar to that of the Spanish CETME
and the Heckler & Koch give the weapon an
extremely light recoil (40% less than the equivalent
bolt action rifle). Apart from the weapon's
outstanding reliability it has been found that during
troop training the average recruit has been able to
shoot more accurately with this weapon than with
the one it replaces. This inherent accuracy and ease
of firing has led to the Swiss adopting the weapon as
a sniper rifle. This in itself is a tremendous
compliment as many countries are forced to employ
a separate bolt-action weapon for sniping use.

SG 510

The SG 510 series of weapons is similar to the
AM55 and is in fact a development of that weapon.
The 510/1 is a standard assault rifle very similar to
the StGw57 but chambered for the NATO 7·62mm
cartridge. The 510/2 is a lightweight version of the
510/1 and is used primarily for paratrooper use. The
510/3 is a lighter weight weapon designed to fire
the 7·62mm short cartridge. This cartridge was
developed from the standard Russian 7·62mm. Its
smaller size and reduction in recoil contributes to the
above reduction in weight. The weapon can be fired
either semi- or fully-automatically and is fed from a
30-round box magazine. It has a cyclic rate of
450-600 rounds per minute and has a muzzle
velocity of 2300fps with a recoil at the shoulder of

The SIG SG510-1 standard
automatic rifle shown here
fitted with the bipod   (*SIG*)

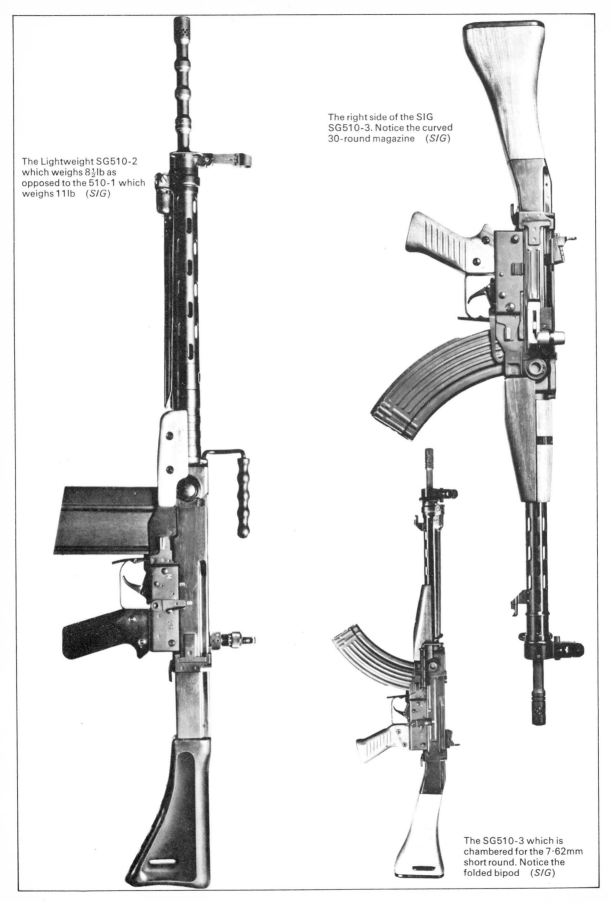

The Lightweight SG510-2 which weighs 8½lb as opposed to the 510-1 which weighs 11lb   (*SIG*)

The right side of the SIG SG510-3. Notice the curved 30-round magazine   (*SIG*)

The SG510-3 which is chambered for the 7·62mm short round. Notice the folded bipod   (*SIG*)

The SIG 510-4 shown fitted with infra-red sniper equipment. It is commendable that the accuracy in a standard weapon makes it suitable for this purpose *(SIG)*

The SG510-4 shown fitted with bipod and telescopic sight *(SIG)*

The right side of the 510-4 shown here with bipod and bayonet fitted *(SIG)*

only 2ft/lbs. As with the StGw57 a variety of accessories can be fitted. One very important advantage from the spare parts problem is that no fitting is needed as all are 100% interchangeable. Needless to say this can only be achieved by the exceedingly high standard of manufacture that is typical of SIG. The main dimensions are : Length 887mm (35 inches) Barrel Length 420mm (16½ inches) Weight (with bipod) 4000g (8lbs 13ozs) and without bipod 3750g (8lbs 4ozs). The SG510/4 is chambered for the standard NATO calibre 7·62 and is the present standard weapon of the Chilean Army, Airforce and Police, and the Bolivian Army. The weapon itself is similar to the 510/3 and as with all 510 weapons utilises the roller lock system. The main dimensions are :— Length 1015mm (40 inches) Barrel Length 505mm (19·9 inches) Weight (without bipod) 4250g (9lbs 6ozs) and with bipod 4450g (9lbs 13ozs). The cyclic rate of fire of 500-650 rpm is achieved and the muzzle velocity is 2600fps. One interesting fact is that the shoulder recoil is 5ft/lbs as compared to only 2ft/lbs of the SG510/3. The muzzle brake integral with the barrel reduces the recoil from

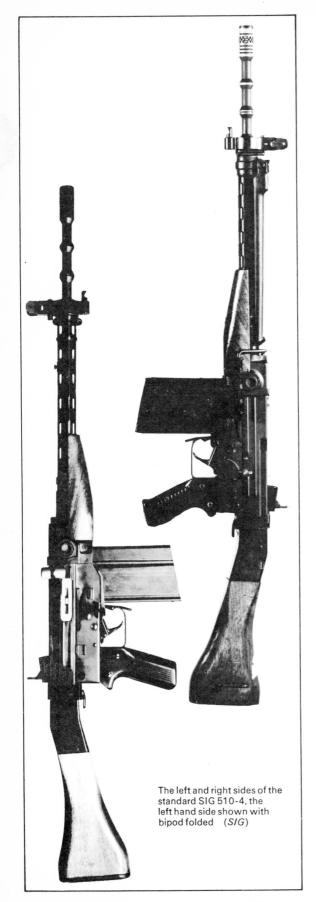

$7\frac{1}{2}$ft/lbs. Once again all the accessories in the range can be fitted to this weapon. A commercial variant of the 510/4 is called the SIG AMT. This weapon is adapted so that only single shots may be fired.

530/1

The 530/1 is a light assault rifle developed to handle such cartridges as the ·223 Armalite or the 7·62mm × 39mm Russian. As the firm of Beretta had been engaged in manufacturing parts of the SG510/4 in 7·62mm from 1961 to 1964 it was natural that the SIG Company should develop the SG530/1 in conjunction with them. This arrangement came to an end when there was a disagreement over whether the weapon was to fire from an open or closed bolt and the type of locking

The retracting stock version of the SIG 510-4 shown with stock retracted. Notice the folded bipod (*SIG*)

The left and right sides of the standard SIG 510-4, the left hand side shown with bipod folded (*SIG*)

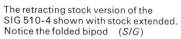

The retracting stock version of the
SIG 510-4 shown with stock extended.
Notice the folded bipod   (*SIG*)

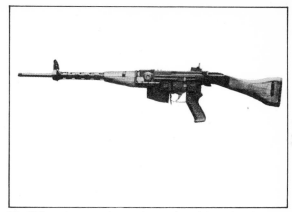

The SIG semi-automatic sporting version of the 510-4   (*SIG*)

A prototype SIG automatic rifle. This
weapon is gas operated   (*SIG*)

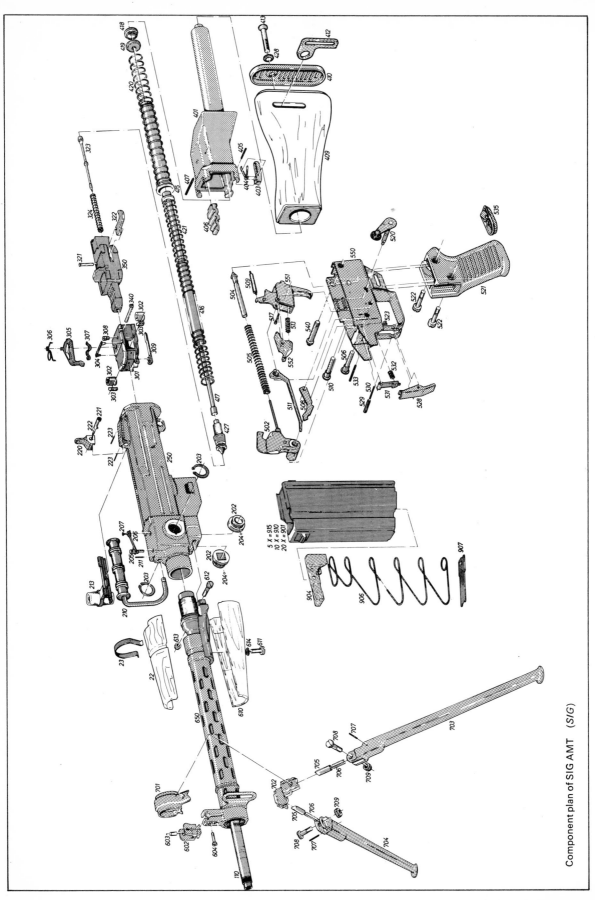

Component plan of SIG AMT (*SIG*)

The SIG SG530-1 left side   (*SIG*)

A further version of the SG530-1. This is a later type weapon   (*SIG*)

system to be employed. SIG wanted to employ the roller lock system used on the 510 but Beretta wanted to use a gas system. The early prototypes were of the roller lock type but after the disagreement SIG decided on a compromise arrangement. This was to use the roller lock but control the rollers by a gas piston assembly.

The main reasons for the adoption of the gas system were firstly that the cook-off limit (the point where the cartridge will detonate by reason of the residue heat in the chamber) which was normally set at 150-160 rounds was found to be not more than 90-100 rounds with the ·223 cartridge ; this was obviously unacceptable. The other and most important problem with a delayed blowback roller type system is that the cases tend to suffer from a head separation problem. A delayed blowback system e.g. the roller system, has the disadvantage that with a high power cartridge the delay is very small and the initial extraction takes place at high speed when the residual pressure is still high. The pressure tends to hold the case against the chamber walls, with the result that the extractor tears the case head off. The use of a fluted chamber to float the case off the chamber walls by bleeding gas down the sides of the case, is one cure and is used by SIG on the 510. The use of a gas system allows the initial extraction to be slowed and thus the danger of case separation is avoided. The SIG 530 combines the roller delay blowback system with the gas system. The gas piston assembly controls the rollers and apart from the advantage already mentioned it allows a gas system to be used without a regulator by virtue of the

tolerance of the roller system to different types of ammunition.

The action of the weapon is held locked by the rollers until gas bled off from the barrel drives the gas piston rearward. It in turn hits the bars controlling the locking rollers taking them out of engagement, thus allowing the bolt assembly to move rearward.

The dimensions of the 530/1 are :
Overall length 37½ inches Barrel length 15·4 inches Overall weight 7lbs 8ozs. It has a cyclic rate of 600rpm on fully automatic fire and the bullet has a muzzle velocity of 2850fps. Once again a number of accessories can be fitted, a folding-stock version is available and rifle grenades can be fired from the standard weapon.

SIG have also experimented with a cartridge

The latest development SIG SG540. Left side (*SIG*)

Notice the difference in barrel and cocking lever in this version of the SG530-1 (*SIG*)

The SG540 shown fully stripped   (*SIG*)

developed by Mauser-IWK which, because of its heavier weight of bullet (a steel core is used) and the designed desire to make it accurate at greater ranges than the Remington round, needs a faster rifling than standard. This is caused by the need to stabilise the bullet, which unfortunately reduces its wounding capability. The increased stability is obtained by changing from the standard one turn in 305mm rifling to one turn in 200mm. This system does not seem to have any overall advantage when the reduced lethal effect is considered, and also the fact that other nations use the standard rifling.

All SIG weapons exhibit superb quality, but whether the price would make them economically the best purchase by other countries is debatable. The fact remains that the SIG rifle is the best finished military weapon available and as efficient as any, and with continued development of new ideas will remain so.

This weapon is not yet in production but will probably succeed the 530/1. The folding stock version of the SG540   (*SIG*)

A SG540 shown fitted with a telescopic sight and bipod. This weapon is designed to fire the short type rifle round   (SIG)

The AR-7. Top picture shows the rifle assembled and the bottom shows it stowed for carriage   (*Author*)

Armalite Weapons

by Major F. W. A. Hobart (Retd.)*

Introduction

Armalite became a Division of Fairchild Engine and Airplane Operation on 1 October 1954. For several years prior to this the Armalite Corporation had been funded privately. The two individuals who started Armalite initially were Charles Dorchester—the present Chairman of the Armalite Board—and George Sullivan a patent counsel who is now connected with Lockheed Aircraft Corporation. Sullivan used his contacts with the late Richard Boutelle president of the Fairchild Engine and Airplane Corporation of Hagerstown Md to get Fairchild interested. The original concept was to produce top quality sporting firearms for the commercial market using advanced designs of light weight, incorporating modern alloys and plastics and making use of the most economical quantity production methods. This plan was changed because of the success achieved by a military venture. Armalite was asked to design a replacement for the standard Air Force survival rifles M4 and M6, and produced the AR-5

·22 Hornet rifle. This design was accepted and designated the MA-1 Survival Rifle in 1955. (No rifles were purchased in quantity due to the large stocks of M4 and M6 rifles held by the Air Force). This early success led to the decision to postpone commercial ventures until the Armalite Division had established its reputation—and improved its financial standing—with military sales, and for the next five years all activity was concentrated on military projects.

One of the first acts of the new Armalite Division of Fairchild was to engage Eugene Stoner, a former Marine, as Chief Engineer. Stoner has proved himself to be one of the foremost armament designers of the century. During his period with the company, 1954-1961 Stoner worked with L. James Sullivan (not to be confused with George Sullivan already mentioned) a talented designer and Robert Fremont who was responsible for design tolerance studies required for mass production.

The following Armalite weapons have been produced. The three most important are the AR-10, AR-15 and AR-18 which will be described in greater detail later.

---

* The views expressed are those of the author and do not reflect official opinion.

AR-1

Work started in 1947, some years before Stoner joined Armalite, and was completed in 1954. This weapon was called the 'Parasniper Rifle' and it was designed to be used either as a military or a high quality sporting rifle, using the 7·62mm NATO cartridge or any convenient sporting round with about the same characteristics. It was a bolt operated rifle with a steel lined aluminium alloy barrel. The stock was of fibre glass foam filled. After completion of the prototype it was decided to proceed no further with its development.

AR-3

This was a 7·62mm self-loading rifle with a forward locking Mauser action. It was brought to Armalite by Eugene Stoner when he joined the Company. It had an aluminium body and a fibre glass butt. It was regarded as a test vehicle for certain design features to be incorporated in subsequent models and was never taken beyond the prototype stage.

AR-5

This was built to a broad specification laid down by the United States Air Force for an aircrew survival rifle. It was a bolt operated rifle weighing only 2¾lbs

and had an overall length of 30½ inches. The action, barrel and magazine were readily detachable and fitted into the interior of the hollow fibre glass butt which reduced its stowed length to 14 inches. The weapon would float either assembled for use or packed away into the buttstock. Using the ·22 Hornet cartridge it had a very reasonable performance and grouped into a four inch circle at its maximum effective range of 100 yards. The original Patent No 179499 of 1 Jan 1957 was ascribed to George Sullivan. The AR-5 was designated the MA-1 but was never ordered in quantity due to the large stocks of M4 and M6 Survival Rifles already held by the Air Force.

AR-7

The 'Explorer'. This is a commercial ·22 LR blow back operated sporting rifle. It retains the breakdown characteristics of the AR-5 and packs similarly into the hollow buttstock. Like its predecessor it will float in either configuration. It has a steel lined aluminium alloy barrel and an 8 round box magazine and groups in a 5 inch circle at 100 yards.

The gun weighs 2¾lbs, is 34½ inches overall and when collapsed has an overall length of 16½ inches. When first marketed it sold for $49·95 with extra

The AR-1. The Parasniper. A Mauser action 7·62mm Military or high quality sporting rifle (*Armalite Inc*)

The AR-5 and AR-7. The AR-5 was a bolt operated USAF survival rifle—known as the MA1 using the ·22 Hornet cartridge. The AR-7 is a blow back operated self-loading sporting rifle using the ·22 LR cartridge (*Author*)

magazines at $2·45. It was extremely easy to stow away in a car or aircraft and has sold in large quantities. It is still available and has given a great deal of pleasure to lots of sportsmen at a very low cost. It is currently selling for $59·95

AR-9

A 12 bore automatic shotgun with an aluminium barrel with an integral compensator and an aluminium body. It incorporated the rotating bolt design of the AR-10 and weighed 5½lbs when developed in 1955. It was decided to concentrate on further development—which led to the AR-17— and not to market the gun in its present form.

AR-10

This military rifle was originally designed in 1953 for the 30-06 cartridge and in 1955 it was modified to take the 7·62mm NATO cartridge. It was the first Armalite rifle to dispense with the gas piston and

Right : Eugene Stoner holding the AR-7 rifle   (*Armalite Inc*)

Below : Charles Dorchester—Chairman of Armalite Inc— showing the AR-7 with its barrel, body and magazine inserted in the hollow plastic buttstock   (*Armalite Inc*)

AR-9 shotgun   (*Armalite Inc*)

use direct gas action. In 1956 Fairchild licensed Artillerie-Inrichtingen of Hembrug, Holland, to manufacture. This state arsenal had some difficulty in raising capital to tool up for a weapon that had not been accepted for service with the Dutch armed forces and there was a considerable delay before they were ready to proceed. In the meanwhile there had been a strong sales effort which was largely wasted and sales went to competitors which although both technically less advanced and sometimes inferior in performance, were readily available. In 1959 Colt's Patent Firearms were licensed to manufacture the AR-10A. This had a stronger extractor, an improved magazine layout and a cocking handle placed over the rear of the body. A prototype was produced but Colt's decided the AR-15 had greater market potential and concentrated their efforts on that weapon which incorporated the improvements of the AR-10A. The basic AR-10 was used as the basis of a bipod mounted magazine-fed LMG and a belt-fed LMG which although generally bipod mounted was also seen on a tripod.

AR-11
This was a rifle designed for the high velocity ·222 cartridge. It resembled the AR-3 and had a Garand type safety. It had an excessive rate of fire and with a conventional stock it climbed badly at full automatic. It was basically a test vehicle for the high velocity light bullet and was a forerunner to the AR-15.

AR-12
This was an inexpensive version of the AR-10 rifle and was chambered for the 7·62mm NATO cartridge. It was intended to utilise stampings rather than machined alloy forgings. It was anticipated that production costs would be 50% of those of the AR-10. It never reached the hardware stage.

AR-13
This was a hyper-velocity gun system for aircraft. It was a multi-barrel type weapon.

AR-14
The AR-14 was an auto-loading sporting rifle and was a commercial version of the AR-10. It was designed to utilise a Monte Carlo stock and in appearance was similar to the AR-17, incorporating a streamlined body of much the same

shape. The barrel was of conventional design with iron sights and was chambered for ·308, ·243 and ·358 calibres. It had a two piece stock and forearm.

AR-15
This rifle was designed between 1956-9. It uses the ·223 cartridge. This round was an Armalite designed round using initially a ·222 Remington case with a 55 grain boat tail bullet developed by the Sierra Bullet Co to Armalite's specification. The volume was inadequate to produce the desired velocities and the case was lengthened to increase the internal volume. The cartridge was then known as the ·222 Special. When Remington produced the ·222 Magnum the Armalite cartridge was re-named the ·223 Remington to prevent confusion. The AR-15 is discussed in more detail later. The weapon in its service version is known in the US Army as the M16A1 and in the USAF as the M16.

AR-16
This rifle was developed and prototyped in 1959-60 by the Armalite development staff with Arthur Miller. Eugene Stoner was Chief Engineer. The calibre chosen was the NATO 7·62mm which at this time was without rival. The AR-16 was designed not to replace the M14 in the US Army but to be manufactured by emergent nations to issue to their own armies. With this in mind the emphasis was placed on ease and economy of production using machine tools that could subsequently be employed in the production of agricultural machinery, office machinery and other requirements of a young nation. The AR-16 made use of sheet steel pressings and automatic screw machine operations as much as possible and reduced the need for milling machines to a minimum. This policy was so successful that only the boltcarrier, barrel, barrel extension and a pair of brackets were completely machined and machine finishing was required only for the bolt, extractor and flash suppressor. The gun was gas operated using a conventional piston, operating rod, a rotating bolt lock and a 20 round magazine. The barrel was 20 inches long and the overall length was 44½ inches. In a carbine version it was 36·9 inches long —27 with the butt folded. The standard gun weighed 8·75lb and fired at approx 650 rounds per minute with a choice of semi or auto fire at will. It was a nice looking gun and there appeared to be every prospect of wide sales but the emergence of the

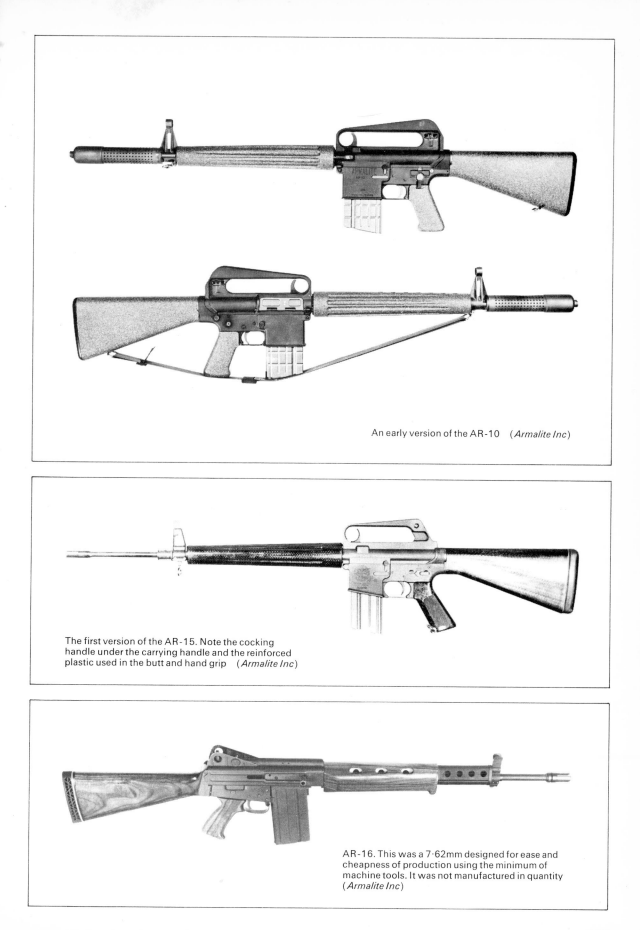

An early version of the AR-10   (*Armalite Inc*)

The first version of the AR-15. Note the cocking handle under the carrying handle and the reinforced plastic used in the butt and hand grip   (*Armalite Inc*)

AR-16. This was a 7·62mm designed for ease and cheapness of production using the minimum of machine tools. It was not manufactured in quantity (*Armalite Inc*)

Carbine version of the AR-16
(*Armalite Inc*)

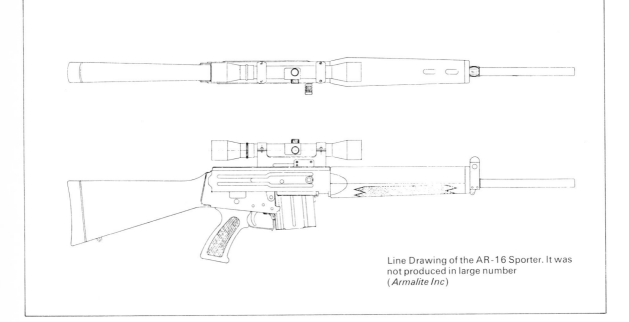

Line Drawing of the AR-16 Sporter. It was
not produced in large number
(*Armalite Inc*)

Colonel Burton T. Miller Vice-President of Armalite with the
AR-17 shotgun   (*Armalite Inc*)

5·56mm cartridge led to the interest of potential
customers switching to the smaller calibre and
Armalite decided to produce a ·223 version which in
due course became the AR-18. An AR-16 sporter
was proposed but was never in large scale
production.

AR-17

The 'golden gun'. This is a commercial 12 bore
automatic 2 shot shotgun—usually supplied in a
golden anodized finish. A black finish is also
available. Using the experience gained with the
AR-9, the very strong multi lug locking system of
the military weapons, is employed. The bolt and
chamber are of steel but the barrel and body are of
7001 aluminium alloy with a claimed ultimate
tensile stress of 70,000psi. The butt and forearm are
made of polycarbonate plastic. It is a recoil operated
arm and so the force exerted on the firer's shoulder
is less than that experienced with a conventional
double-barrelled shotgun. The barrel is 24 inches in

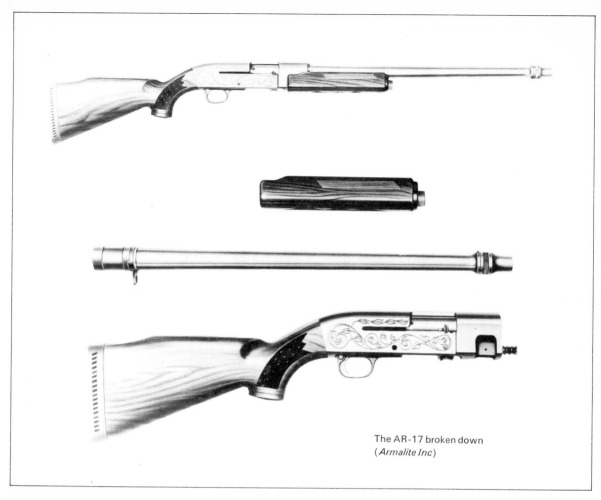

The AR-17 broken down
(*Armalite Inc*)

The locking system of the AR-17 came from the AR-16   (*Armalite Inc*)

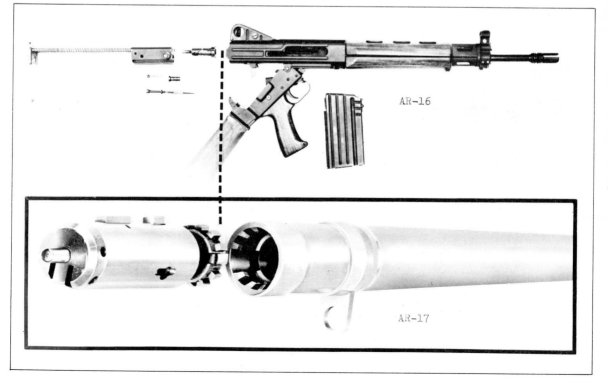

AR-16

AR-17

length and three choke tubes—modified, improved cylinder and full choke—are supplied with each gun. The gun not only caters for the normal shot but by making provision for the addition of weights both in the stock and forearm, allows the enthusiast to vary the position of the centre of gravity to suit his individual requirements.

The gun weighs 5·6lb and is 45 inches long assembled—24 inches when taken down. The body is 10 inches. There is a rubber recoil pad on the butt. When first marketed in 1964 it cost $159·50.

AR-18

This came out in 1964 after two years of development subsequent to the finalisation of the basic design. It is a ·223 version of the AR-16 with the same virtues of simplicity, economy and ease of production. In 1967 the Howa Machinery Company of Nagoya, Japan, started production but the program encountered difficulty when the Japanese Government would not permit exports to any country remotely involved in the Vietnam conflict. When a number were required for US testing, the

Loading the AR-17. A two shot automatic recoil operated shotgun largely made of aluminium alloy   (*Armalite Inc*)

The AR-18. An inexpensive, accurate, sturdy ·223 military rifle with a straight through design producing accurate fire both at single-shot and full-auto (*Author*)

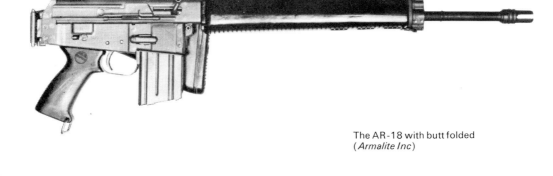

The AR-18 with butt folded (*Armalite Inc*)

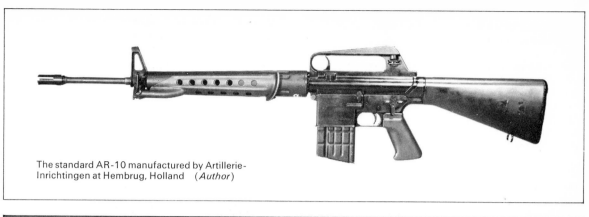

The standard AR-10 manufactured by Artillerie-Inrichtingen at Hembrug, Holland   (*Author*)

The body and selector switch of the Dutch AR-10 (*Armalite Inc*)

Japanese Government denied Howa permission to supply them and the gun is now also in production by Armalite Inc at Costa Mesa in California. The Japanese Government subsequently approved delivery of AR-18 rifles to European, Latin American and even some non-combatant Asian countries.

AR-180
This is a self loading version of the AR-18 designed for sporting use and employment by police forces. It has a modified trigger mechanism embodying seven changes to make it impossible for anyone to convert it to full auto, and to conform with US regulations features a reduced capacity magazine. Howa Machinery Company is presently manufacturing the AR-180 and delivering to Armalite for sale in the United States and other countries.

The AR-10
The feature of greatest interest in this gun is the gas system. The earliest designers of automatic weapons Maxim, Browning and Von Odkolek all became interested in gas operated weapons. Maxim obtained a British patent for a short stroke piston adaption of a Martini-Henry but concentrated largely on recoil operation and did not pursue the line of his patent. Browning evolved the swinging arm method in his 'potato-digger' in the Colt model 1895 and Von Odkolek sold his patents to Hotchkiss who produced a gas piston operated model in 1895.

The first 'direct action' gas system—eliminating the piston altogether was designed by Llunjman—a Swedish engineer. It was incorporated in the Halvautomatiski Gever Ag-42, a rifle firing the Swedish 6·5mm cartridge. The principle was used in the Madsen-Llunjman rifle, later the Hakim rifle and in the French MAS 59. From this it can be seen that the AR-10 followed a well tried pattern in which gas tapped off from the barrel flows back along a tube and produces a force to unlock the bolt. In the AR-10 the gas passes along a stainless steel tube and enters a space within the cylindrical shell of the bolt carrier. Here it forces the carrier back. After about $\frac{1}{8}$in of free travel to allow the chamber pressure to fall, a cam path cut in the carrier causes a pin on the bolt to revolve about the longitudinal axis of the bolt and thus rotates the bolt locking lugs out of engagement with the barrel extension. The carrier then pulls the bolt bodily to the rear to start the operating cycle. There is no primary extraction and the empty case is pulled sharply out of the chamber and ejected from the gun. The bolt carrier stores energy in the return spring and comes forward again to chamber a round from the 20 round box magazine. When the cartridge is fully chambered

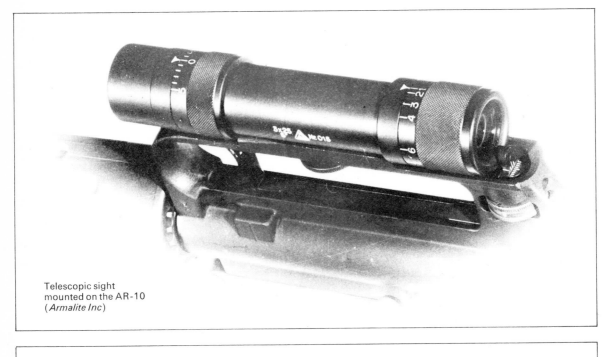

Telescopic sight mounted on the AR-10 (*Armalite Inc*)

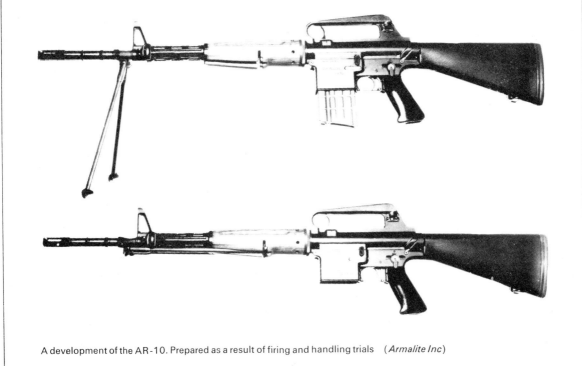

A development of the AR-10. Prepared as a result of firing and handling trials   (*Armalite Inc*)

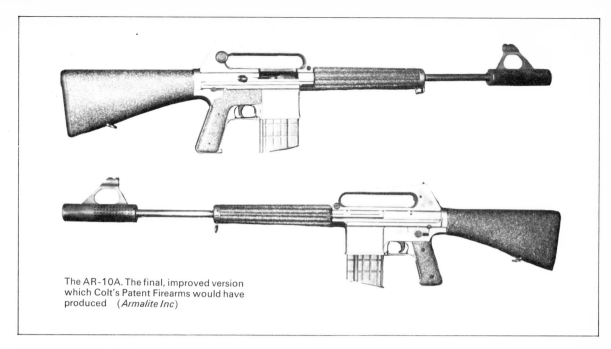

The AR-10A. The final, improved version which Colt's Patent Firearms would have produced   (*Armalite Inc*)

The AR-10 belt fed mounted on a tripod. The belt can just be seen feeding into the right hand side   (*Armalite Inc*)

Barrel changing on the machine gun version of the AR-10 (*Armalite Inc*)

the seven locking lugs on the bolt head are rotated through $22\frac{1}{2}$ degrees and lock behind abutments in the barrel extension. The hammer cannot be released until locking is completed. The weapon will fire at either single shot or full automatic with a selector lever on the left of the body. The aperture back sight is in the rear pillar of the carrying handle and is raised or lowered by a horizontal drum graduated from 200 to 700m by 100m divisions. Stripping the AR-10 is a simple matter. After the gun is made safe a pin located at the rear of the body is pulled out. The upper receiver then pivots up and the bolt and carrier assembly can be withdrawn and separated.

The AR-10 features the use of alloy forgings in the two parts of the receiver, fibreglass pistol grip and a

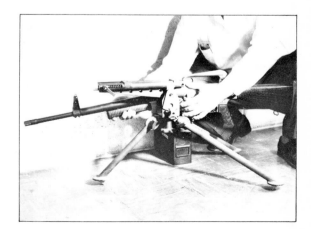

plastic butt. The magazine is of light alloy. These materials allow an unloaded weight of 9·0lb. Some variations on the AR-10 have been made. The principle variations are:

1 Short-barrelled carbine.
2 Magazine-fed LMG.
3 Belt-fed LMG.

None of these is in production.

The AR-10 has been singularly unfortunate in that it was developed when the emphasis was on the change to a smaller calibre and when there was a market the Dutch were very tardy in tooling up. In all only 5000 guns were made by Artillerie-Inrichtingen. Thus a potentially good gun never saw service.

The AR-15

The ·223 (5·56mm) AR-15 was designed by Eugene Stoner. It uses the same method of gas operation as the AR-10 and, broadly, is derived from that gun. To understand the reason for the adoption of this gun it is necessary to be aware of the user's needs. The Infantry Board, Fort Benning laid down the following as its requirement:

1 Loaded weight not to exceed 6lb.
2 Accuracy and maximum height of trajectory to be at least equal to that of the M1 rifle at ranges up to 500 yards.
3 Selective fire capability.
4 Penetration of body armour, steel helmet or 10 gauge steel plate at 500 yards.
5 Lethality not less than the M1 carbine at 500 yards.

These led to the design of a lightweight low impulse rifle firing a lightweight bullet at high velocity. No round of a suitable type existed so Armalite had to start by obtaining a cartridge. Whether the calibre and weight—·223in and 55 grains—selected were the best possible, is open to debate. In retrospect a calibre of ·26 and perhaps 80 grains would have produced a round which could have the range and lethality required for a light machine gun. As a result of the requirements and the acquisition of a cartridge the AR-10 was scaled down for testing. The earliest prototypes even had the cocking handle on top of the body. Ten AR-15 rifles were delivered to the Infantry Board on 31 March 1958. They were tested at Aberdeen Proving Ground with satisfying results and the Board recommended that the AR-15 be considered as a replacement for the M14 7·62mm rifle. After arctic tests at Fort Greely modifications were made including strengthening the barrel to allow for firing with water in the bore, the trigger guard was modified to allowing firing in arctic mittens and the cocking handle was removed from inside the carrying handle and located behind it. Various other tests followed and a procurement programme started. The US Air Force was very interested and Lt-Col Burton T. Miller, then serving, tested the AR-15. The Air Force took 8500 in 1961, the Army took 85,000 in the same year followed by 85,000 in 1963, 35,000 in 1964, 100,000 in 1965 and a further 100,000 in 1966. The Vietnam

struggle undoubtedly increased the demand. Colt's Patent Firearms Company had been licensed to produce the gun in January 1959 and they manufactured the quantities mentioned. On 30 June 1967 the US Government and Colt made a contract whereby the Government agreed to pay $4,500,000 for a license to use technical data and all patents relating to the M16 rifle. This enabled them to set up additional production from other firms and both General Motors and Harrington and Richardson have each manufactured the AR-15.

The original AR-15 was designated the M16. The Air Force version still has this nomenclature but the Army rifle was modified in 1966 to become the M16E1 and in 1967 this became the M16A1. The differences are chiefly that the M16A1 has a bolt with serrations on the right hand side and a plunger protruding from the body can be used to force the bolt home if the return spring for some reason is unable to do so. This device allows the firer to close his bolt when a dirty cartridge produces a high friction force and thus saves fitting a reciprocating cocking handle such as that used on the Russian AKM. Whether such a device is correct in principle is doubtful, because eventually forcing rounds into the chamber ignores the reason for the difficult chambering and may result in scoring the chamber, feeding a malformed cartridge or otherwise damaging the mechanism.

The original AR-15 had a twist of rifling of one turn in 14 inches. An unclassified US report produced by the Ballistics Laboratory entitled 'Exterior Ballistics of the AR-15 Rifle' showed that although the bullet was marginally stable in air at 60°F, when fired in Arctic conditions the bullet was totally unstable. This led to the production of a twist of one turn in 12 inches and with this increased rotation of the bullet it is now just stable at below zero air temperatures. This has resulted in some loss of lethality but not to a significant degree.

When the M16 was initially issued to troops in Vietnam—and particularly to the US Marines—they were told that the gun was self-cleaning. A spate of complaints about the case failing to eject led to a Congressional Enquiry. The causes were found to be associated with an unannounced change from tubular IMR propellant to ball propellant, and lack of cleaning. There is no doubt that ball powder does have several different effects to IMR. Chiefly, these are an increased rate of fire and depositions of fouling in the cavity between the bolt carrier and the bolt head. This carbon when hot is soft but after a short while it cools and hardens to produce a bond strong enough to prevent the bolt unlocking; nor can the rifle be hand operated. As a result the weapon became inoperative. Following from this enquiry several changes were made.

The soldier was issued with a cleaning kit, the buffer was modified to reduce the rate of fire and the chamber was chromium plated. The net effect of these innovations was to produce a rifle which now is at least as reliable as any other in service. Technically the AR-15 is much the same as the AR-10. It uses the direct gas action system and the same bolt system as its predecessor and has the

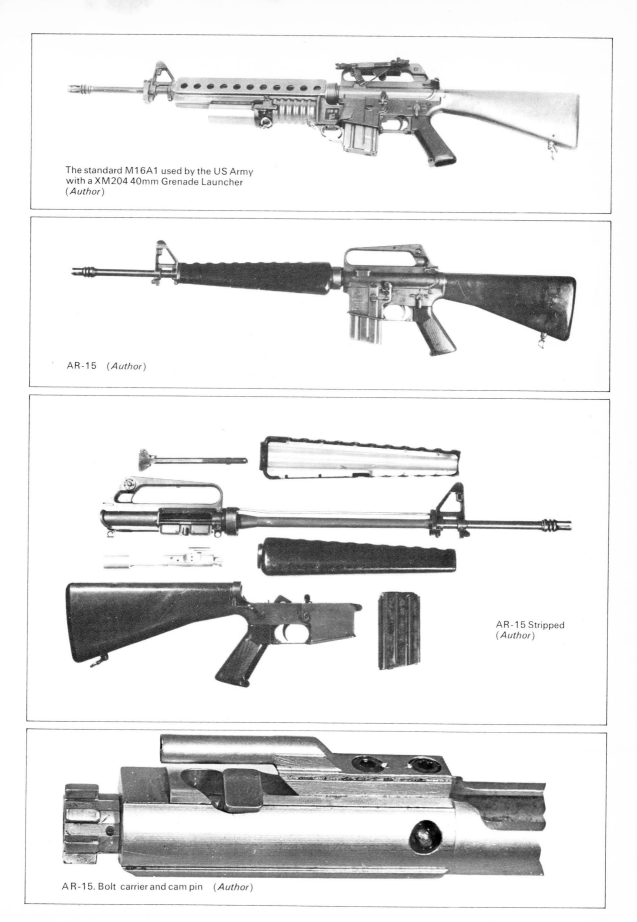

The standard M16A1 used by the US Army
with a XM204 40mm Grenade Launcher
(*Author*)

AR-15   (*Author*)

AR-15 Stripped
(*Author*)

AR-15. Bolt carrier and cam pin   (*Author*)

same butt giving a straight through action and thus reducing the tendency for the muzzle to rise at full automatic fire.

There is a civilian version firing as a self loading sporting rifle, known as the Colt Commanche. This name was later dropped due to objection by an Aircraft Manufacturer already using that name. There are also various military adaptations. These include a heavy barrelled version known as the Colt Automatic Rifle which can be magazine fed (M1) or a later version belt fed (M2). Both are bipod mounted. There is also the Colt Commando which is a short-barrelled version of the AR-15 with a very practical telescoping butt stock, designed as a submachine gun and used extensively in Vietnam by the Green Berets, the Special Forces Unit of the US Army.

The AR-18

In early 1961 Eugene Stoner left Armalite and became a consultant working with Colt, Cadillac Gage and on the TMW 25mm cannon.

The AR-18 was not his work but was designed after Armalite separated from Fairchild Aeroplane Company in 1961. (Arthur Miller was Armalite's Chief Engineer after Stoner left.) The patents for this gun are registered in the names of Miller, Dorchester and Sullivan. (The connection of the two latter named with Armalite has already been mentioned.) The AR-18 comes directly from the AR-16 which fired the 7·62mm NATO round and was never produced in quantity as interest in most countries was beginning to be directed to the ·223in round. It is, I think, true to say that the AR-18 owes something to nearly all of its Armalite successors

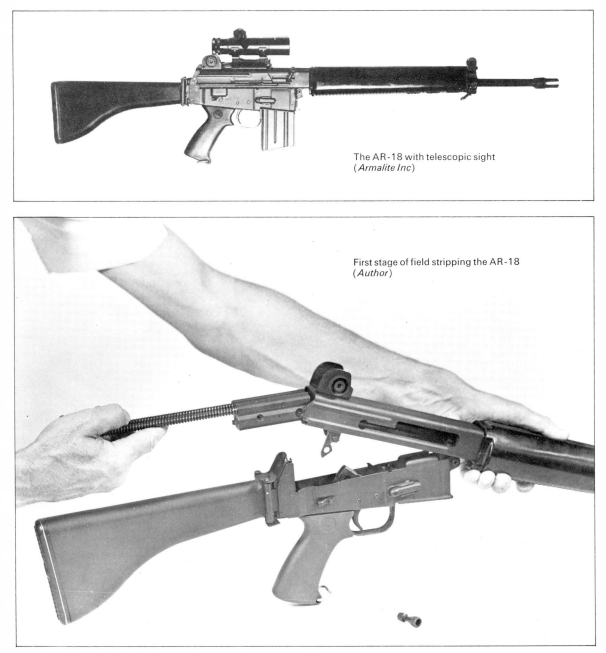

The AR-18 with telescopic sight
(*Armalite Inc*)

First stage of field stripping the AR-18
(*Author*)

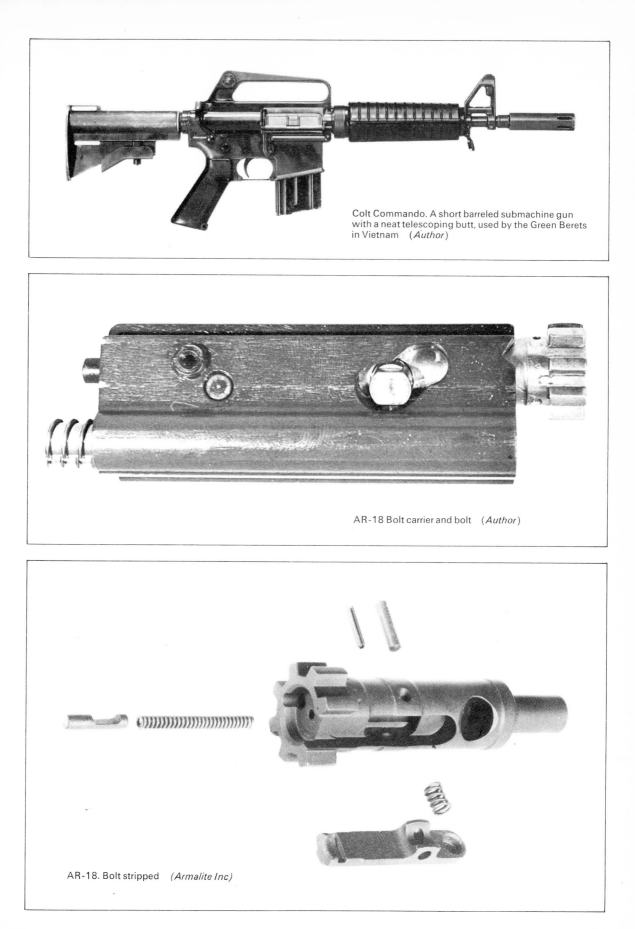

Colt Commando. A short barreled submachine gun with a neat telescoping butt, used by the Green Berets in Vietnam   (*Author*)

AR-18 Bolt carrier and bolt   (*Author*)

AR-18. Bolt stripped   (*Armalite Inc*)

but in particular it was designed for simple, cheap quantity production by countries with limited facilities. The manufacturer says that it is produced from 14 stampings, 28 automatic screw machine operations, three machined castings, six mouldings, and four machined parts. These latter are the barrel, barrel extension, bolt carrier and extractor. Springs, washers, pins etc are bought out from commercial firms. The gun uses steel stampings instead of the alloy forgings of the AR-15. Armalite state that a run of 50,000 AR-18s is required to justify, economically, local production. This is less than any comparable weapon.

System of Operation
The weapon is gas-operated with a vent located $12\frac{3}{4}$in from the breech face and $5\frac{3}{8}$in from the muzzle. The cylinder is of stainless steel mounted above the barrel with $\frac{3}{16}$in clearance. It is $1\frac{3}{8}$in long. The cylinder takes the form of a hollow spigot over which fits a female piston $1\frac{7}{8}$in long. The male member has a gas ring around the end. When the piston has moved back $\frac{1}{2}$in, four vents pass over the gas ring and the gas is evacuated under the top of the fore grip. Thus the working impulse is imparted to the piston over only $\frac{1}{8}$in travel. The actuating rod is in two parts ; a short head 1in long which fits into the main rod $9\frac{7}{8}$in in length. This rod has a collar $3\frac{3}{4}$in from the end which forms the forward housing of the actuating rod return spring. This short stroke piston action is similar in design principle to that of the German war-time Gewehr 43. There is no gas regulator. The rod is in contact with the top of the front face of the bolt carrier and in its $\frac{1}{2}$in movement imparts enough energy for the completion of the entire cycle of operations.
The bolt head carries seven locking lugs which are rotated for locking through $22\frac{1}{2}°$ to engage in front of corresponding locking shoulders in the barrel extension. On the shaft of the bolt is a pin which projects to enter a cam way on the carrier. When the carrier moves back impelled by the piston thrust, the pin first moves across the width of the camway—a distance of $\frac{1}{8}$in—to provide mechanical safety, and is then forced down to rotate and unlock the bolthead. The pin rides in a spot welded guideway which prevents any movement. The continued rearward movement of the carrier pulls the bolt with it to the rear. The extractor is mounted at 3 o'clock on the bolt face and withdraws the empty case which is ejected through an opening on the right of the receiver by the action of a spring-loaded plunger set in the bolt face at 9 o'clock which acts as soon as the case is free of the barrel extension. The bolt moves back along two guide rods which pass through it, compressing the two return springs mounted around the rods.
On the forward movement of the carrier the lowest of the bolt locking lugs pushes the top round of the 20 in the magazine forward and it is guided up into the chamber. The bolt reaches the limit of its forward travel and is then rotated to lock by the action of the camway on the pin. After locking is completed the carrier travels forward a further $\frac{1}{8}$in to provide mechanical safety before firing. Until this last $\frac{1}{8}$in is completed the firing pin mounted in the carrier

cannot reach the cap. The firing pin is strongly spring retracted and so 'g' forces cannot produce an unintentional firing—as was the case in the early AR-15 which had a heavy free-floating pin.

Trigger and Firing Mechanism
The weapon will fire at either single shot or full automatic.

Full Auto
Lying along the bottom of the receiver is a spring-loaded rod which at its front end carries a vertical hook which is driven forward by the bolt carrier as locking is completed. This forward movement rotates the automatic sear backwards and releases the hammer. Thus the weapon can only fire when locking is completed. Pulling the trigger lowers the trigger extension which is engaged on a bent on an extension of the hammer below its axis pin. This fires the first shot. Thereafter firing is controlled, whilst the trigger remains pressed, by the spring-loaded rod which activates the automatic or 'safety' sear.

Single Shot
The trigger extension releases the hammer and the round is fired. The hammer comes back and through a hole in it passes a secondary sear which is spring-loaded and grips the front edge of the aperture in the hammer. The trigger must be released to free this sear and the hammer is then gripped by the trigger extension. This in principle is an adaptation of the double bent system used on the Garand and M14. Putting the change lever to 'semi' rotates the spindle which holds the safety sear out of operation. This means that the trigger can be operated with the bolt only partially forward. The gun is completely safe because the hammer energy is then used to close the bolt and a misfire results.

Safety
The hammer must be cocked before the safety can be applied. The change lever spindle forces the secondary sear down and locks it. At the same time it rotates over a backward extension of the trigger and locks that.
In general it is a very pleasant weapon to handle and fire. It is accurate and consistent. There is a submachine gun version with a shortened barrel and also a self loading sporter rifle known as the Armalite AR-180 which has received very favourable comment in the US magazines.

Conclusions
Prior to World War II nearly all design, development and production in the USA was concentrated in the Arsenals.
The Armalite Corporation has shown that private enterprise can do a fine job and in producing the AR-15 at the crucial moment when the inadequacies of the M14 were very apparent, it stepped into the role of provider for the US Forces in Vietnam.
When the time comes for the next generation of rifles to be adopted Armalite will doubtless have something ready for consideration.

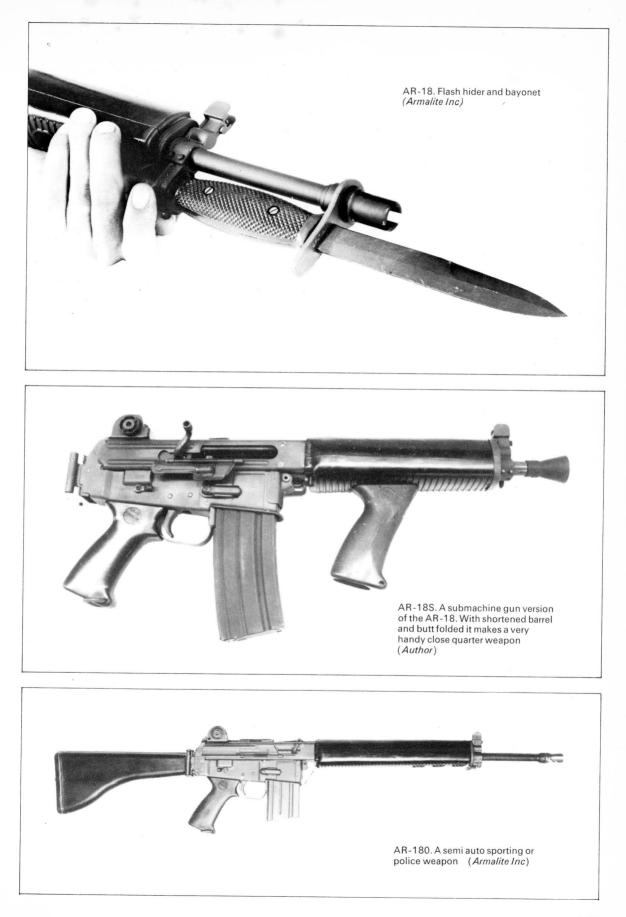

AR-18. Flash hider and bayonet
(*Armalite Inc*)

AR-18S. A submachine gun version
of the AR-18. With shortened barrel
and butt folded it makes a very
handy close quarter weapon
(*Author*)

AR-180. A semi auto sporting or
police weapon   (*Armalite Inc*)

ARMALITE WEAPONS COMPARATIVE TABLE

	AR-10	AR-15	AR-18
Calibre	7·62mm NATO	·223in	·223in
Type of Ammunition	Any approved NATO	Remington, Norma, Federal etc	Remington, Norma, Federal etc
Muzzle Energy	2340ft lb	1285ft lb	1285ft lb
Recoil Energy	10½ft lb	4·4ft lb	4·13ft lb
Muzzle Velocity	2750ft/s	3250ft/s	3250ft/s
Overall length	40½in	38⅜in	38⅜in
Length stock retracted	—	—	29in
Weight empty	9·0lb	6·5lb	7·0lb
Weight with full 20 rd magazine	10·6lb	7·25lb	7·75lb
Barrel length	20in	20in	18¼in
No of grooves	4	6	6
Direction of Twist	RH	RH	RH
Pitch of Twist	1 in 10in	1 in 12in	1 in 12in
Locking	Rotating bolt	Rotating bolt	Rotating bolt
Gas system	Direct action	Direct action	Piston
Sights			
Front	Fixed blade	Cylindrical post	Cylindrical post
Rear	Aperture 200-700	Aperture Flip	Aperture 200 and 400 Flip
Windage	Nil	Variable plate	Milled knob
Zeroing	Elevation—Rear sight	Elevation—Foresight	Elevation—Foresight
	Line—Rear sight	Line—Foresight	Line—Windage scale
Sightbase	20¾in	20in	19½ and 20in
Effective Range			
Single shot	400m	400m	400m
Full auto	150m	300m	300m
Rate of Fire			
Single shot	40rpm	40rpm	40rpm
Auto (bursts)	80rpm	80rpm	80rpm
Cyclic	700rpm	650-850rpm	800rpm

AR-18S. Photograph showing accuracy and penetration achieved at 300 and 365 yards (*Armalite Inc*)

Small Arms Editor: A. J. R. Cormack